Prarthana

The Prayers–
A Book on Munduka and on Open Meditation

notionpress.com

Prarthana

The Prayers–
A Book on Munduka and on Open Meditation

A M Nagesh

notionpress.com

Notion Press

Old No. 38, New No. 6

McNichols Road, Chetpet

Chennai - 600 031

First Published by Notion Press 2016

ISBN 978-93-5206-867-8

Dedicated to

My Family

QUOTE

Unless humanity does not act as fuel, unless humility does not possess the power of engine and unless humbleness does not steer the goodness among the people, the human accent is a far cry.

CONTENTS

PREFACE

The changes in the law of the land cause powerful psycho-social signatories to turn a blind eye to the pain and sorrows of the world's human salvo, with no solution forthcoming. The erroneous values and fraudulent virtues of the ever-growing political power have sharpened the edges of psycho-social unrest, represented as a knife. This knife has extremely sharp edges that have left today's men maimed and soaked with blood. Though recovery could be possible, it is farfetched due to man made demarcations, not as borders but deep in the peoples' heart. The unrest in Central America is for control over the Drug Lords; in certain parts of Africa, the War Lords claim the supremacy of anarchist states; in south west Asia, they proclaim it as a religious state, butchering, sabotaging and beheading the democratic values of the world, driving the innocent to the neighbouring states only to add cultural chaos after unabated exodus. The refugees are stranded with unseen human tragedies, and with profound psychological turmoil in the refugee camps.

The millions of people in the coastal region have troubled hearts, as they are waiting until they have a final glimpse of their only home that might submerge due to the rising levels of the ocean, due to the rise in temperature, melting ice caps and disappearing polar glaciers. It is not too far for us to hear fading songs of exotic birds as the aftermath of deforestation, as the great Amazon would witness. The El Niño effect, whether natural or man made, makes humans suffer with torrential rains in one corner of the earth, deadly winds in another far-off corner, and causing cascading draught in the centre of certain part of the world. The grain sowed in the fields produced no yield, and this made us witnesses to stranded farmers, with no other choice than to commit suicide, as their debts kept mounting. The natural catastrophic disasters on periodical basis have left trails of destructions and thus human sufferings.

The enormous promises in the high-profile political rallies led the countrymen to despair, as they were not fulfilled. Innumerable country partisans of varied languages had frequent frictions along the borders, with arson and riots, regarding the establishment of their languages. Daggers piercing deep into religious hearts along religious lines lead to violence with disastrous ends. The constant friction between politicians and the judiciary has created a vacuum to fill the truth and fair Judgments. Our country's intelligentsia with pseudo-secularist faces have caused deep wounds in the majority of intelligent youth, who wish to build our country to its greatest heights. The recent popular modalities against moral education have led deep indentations in the value system of our country. The wise people are muzzled by the immoral, who are seen silencing their virtues with the sound of guns. The pen trembles, fears and is scared to bring forth the thoughts of the writer, blocking his freedom of speech, and they have buried the same in the graveyards of intellectual burial grounds. The rightists and leftists race to conquer the fundamental rights of the elected democratic body, and we are left with murders and mass killings. Development and technology is as a rose with hidden thorns, which leave many fingers bleeding. Deep divisions along the lines of social inequality, between the rich and poor, keep widening day-by-day, resulting in social unrest with consequent socio legal problems. The increasing population with unparallel male female ratio has made people incompetent with lingering life continuing. Increasing trends of psychopathy, deviancy and mental aberrations have led to torture of toddlers and sexual abuse of children at an alarming frequency. However, the saga of life continues and continues forever, which probably causes each human to fall-back on his discoveries or inventions, to reduce the agony, pain and sorrow.

In this venture, man has found only three things in this world that has universal acceptance. One is love, another is music and the next is meditation. As I know all these three constructs have no known divisions among humans, hence, I presume that they are accepted by mankind. I am neither a spiritualist nor a musician to render pure love or only music, respectively. In my thirty-two years of psychiatric practice, I have seen and felt the subtle pain people undergo. Hence, being a treating psychiatrist, I am able to offer a new method of meditation, and probably practicing my new meditation would give remedy to a reader's stressful mind.

Day-by-day the medical profession has become expensive, to enrol in a medical course or to furnish treatment for these patients at low cost. The peoples' affordability for tertiary health care is reducing. The government is doing everything possible to increase its allocation on health and is trying to implement it by the plastic card culture (various insurance policies, government and semi-private). By doing so, the patient and doctor relationship is shrinking day-by-day. I am yet to know a man who for his mistake is born into this wonderful world as a nerd or, there is some error in rendering the basic needs by these stingy need providers. Extensive thinking has created a frightening atmosphere for a thinker. This is the reason why I thought to search for that which is there already in our ancient scriptures, and to bring to the masses my concept of Open Meditation, to reduce their stress, to acknowledge their boredoms and to move forward in understanding the realms of life. I hope the reader, after reading my concept of Open Meditation, finds help and is able to throw some light on the causes of his stress.

MUNDKUA

What actually fascinated me was why people throng temples to offer their hair (tonsure) to God? As a result of my inquisitiveness, I tried to squeeze out certain answers from my friends and pundits. All of them had their own prejudiced answers to my question, and I was not satisfied. Some of them narrated their own explanations regarding the miraculous benefits a person would get from this ritual. Many answers I got from them were on the "belief" factor. According to me, this "belief" is a subjective instrument, which works within one's own psychological sphere. It is unlike "faith," which is a par below word meant for religious people; faith does not get individualized, because "faith" belongs to a group of individuals. As I do not belong to any concocted religion, this faith does not affect me. I have only one faith. My faith is to believe in myself. I personally presume that his "belief" is a word, which suits well within the corporate psyche. We as simple men who want to try these "belief" games with business minds feel more complex in understanding. The reason would be that complexity of these games that people play is internal or within. The games that the corporate organisations play would be in collusion with people having ill-gotten wealth and dishonest politicians; hence, these games seem complicated to comprehend. In reality, "belief" transactions are murkier, a totally dirty merchandise.

Hence, this could be the sole reason for me to "believe" in myself rather than on someone else or "belief", in God.

When I try to meditate on "belief," this "belief", is a 916 Hall Mark for a thriving person or for that matter to an enterprising man who mesmerizes his clients to believe him. Hence, the word, "belief," is prerogative to one's personal skill. Here, I would like to narrate the paradox nature of this word "belief." For an ignorant and innocent humble man, "belief" is everything. His belief in God would bring him much-needed happiness. His belief in his employer would bring much-needed increments in his salary. A student's belief on his teacher would bring him the required knowledge. To make it simpler, we feel that simply believing in someone would bring all happiness in our life. According to me, this particular statement is a myth. Whatever belief a person might harbour, his individual success is because of his pure application in the business he does. His achievements are achieved by his skill and perseverance. The "skill" I mention here does not come under the four common functions of our brain. The normal core functions of our brain are the following: Thinking, will, feeling and work.

These four functions have been humbly gifted by the creator to man for a simple living, reasonable success and for his race to propagate. Hence, "skill" is anthropologically and also evolutionally a new word. Nowadays, it is well established by neuro-psycholinguists that skill is one among the many cognitive functions of the brain. This is exactly why I call this, "belief," as a part and parcel of corporate vocabulary. After believing this word, "belief," there might be two paths that a man could experience in his achievements. One is by believing that as a person he could excel and second could be that he could fall as a prey to someone else.

I am a psychiatrist; hence, I use this word "belief" very often to my patients in my counselling sessions. I really do not know whether their belief in me works wonders to treat their symptoms or their belief in themselves cured the symptoms. From this dichotomy, it is clear that "belief" is always a business word in this world of financial give and take policy. We just believe on the advertisements while purchasing some goods. After purchasing the aforesaid goods, it is our luck if at all everything goes fine, but when the same goods start giving trouble, then the luck lies with the company, hence a man who had purchased goods would be a worried man harbouring irritability and anxiety. The purchaser would keep on talking over the phone with service providers hurling abuses or getting abused. The purchaser might even think of suing the company. Hence, after purchasing certain goods, we are at the company's mercy. I have experienced this after purchasing my car. Actually, I had purchased my car on a "Service is our motto, belief is our hall mark" slogan. This "service" and "beliefs" are with them till I had received a letter from their headquarters and I ticked the tab "Excellent services" before mailing.

Sometimes I am in the habit of going for a walk in the morning when I am unable to play tennis. I came across a church named as "Believers Church." I was amazed to read this signboard. This signboard confused me with regard to this "Belief" part. Because, as per my knowledge, Lord Krishna, compassionate Christ and messenger Mohamed never asked their believers to believe in them. The reason could be that all these three Messiahs conveyed or taught us only "good." Anybody who recognizes the "well" in the society refuses to accept the phrase, "You believe me." There could be a circumstance to believe when a person has done something wrong, as somebody has to "believe" him that he has done no wrong. Hence, this "belief" is a tricky word for those who preach "bad" to the society. This is exactly why we blindly believe in many God's all though only one God exists and that God is a good part of oneself.

Until now, the "belief" I am mentioning is all about humans, who are designed to move and talk by the creator. However, what about our belief on super forms that do not talk or walk, the Gods? Should I think my belief is on imagined super forms (with due apology to believers) or on whom I cannot perceive these forms, as "Super Belief." At this juncture, when I was in a state of perplexity, I wanted to find a suitable answer to this "belief" or to someone else's "belief." While searching the truth behind this "belief," I came across the Upanishath. I thought probably by reading and understanding this age old scripture it would throw some light on my messed up Belief.

UPANISHATH

Let me accept that I am not an exponent on the Upanishath or allied branches of ancient scriptures. My reading was just a hobby to overcome the mundane. After thirty-two years of practice in psychiatry, as I turn older, I desire my mind to do some soul searching to overcome my boredom and to engage myself further busily. While doing so, I searched many book stalls and even searched the search engines, including the "Amazon kindle," to find a book on Upanishath, but to my surprise, whatever interesting books on these scriptures I had found were written in English by western authors. The literature that I found by Indian sages on this Upanishath were written in Sanskrit and have been translated in English or in Kannada by few authors. I am not a *Pundit* in Sanskrit. Till my tenth standard, I had studied Sanskrit as a secondary language. Presently, I have vague pictorial sketches of this learnt Sanskrit lurking somewhere in one of the trillions of spaces in my brain memory. Frankly, I could pick up only a small fraction of Sanskrit after I began reading Upanishath. Hence, my knowledge on Upanishath Scriptures is very limited. One thing I would like to highlight here is that each word of Sanskrit is so fascinating because the same word of this mystic language would give myriads of meanings according to its context of usage. I did not find similar message in any other languages unlike that this Sanskrit language possesses.

For example, *Yo Vai* or *Idam Vai* would mean as "This Verily" and it is being used in different contexts in the Sanskrit language. In Kannada, for example, the same would mean "*Suukshma,*" and though this word originated originally from Sanskrit, it would represent many constructs and characters of the functions that our brain possesses, *chitha Dharma* (properties of mind). My previous book was on life's attributes (Paavithratha—the purity, a book on life's attributes). It is relevant to refresh what this "life's attributes" would mean. Let me not go according to any classical English dictionary, but to describe this phrase in simple words is that the "attributes" I have narrated are the sub-atomic psycho-social-materialistic functional strings (Verily) to connect this whole world together for an eluding harmony. The same analogy one could find in particle physics under String Theory. Hence, *Chittha Dharma* is the property of mind but my explanations on life attributes would meet the properties of *Samaja Dharma* (Natural laws of society). Coming to the basis of my narration, "this verily" is a belief that lacks full proof or lacks scientific explanations. I presume that this could be one of the many reasons why the present young generations do not try to delve into the depth of the Upanishath or Puranas. I feel this young generation never relishes reading these scriptures. Invariably, young consider that reading these scriptures is for the intelligentsia and for the knowledgeable retired people. Today, the majority in the young generation also feel that these scriptural themes would rely mainly on "beliefs." Today, all over the world, youth have been termed as "atheists." This attitude is not their problem; this problem actually is because of non-development of certain neuronal tracts in their brains, which could have possessed "believer' functions."

Many *Vaachanas* (discourses) by spiritual Swamys helped listeners to relieve their stress and this is acceptable. When the same discourse ends with a note on "belief," then I am the last person to believe them. This also I presume holds good for the young generation to not believe these types of cock and bull stories. Primarily, a psychiatrist's role while managing his patients, his main aim, is to relieve the patient's anxiety and the ignorance on patient's illnesses. This is the basic principle that a psychiatrist should abide to or by any doctor for that matter.

Let me try to explain what this Upanishath means to me?

The meaning to "*Upa*" is "subsidiary." For example, our neighbouring country, Sri Lanka, is termed as *Upa Kanda* to India. In terms of India's size, Sri Lanka's size is small and it is adjacent, hence *Upa Kanda*. Similarly, "*Nishath*" is mega-library of *Brahman,* for which Upanishath is a small branch or subsidiary to this. Likewise, *Upanyasam* in other words is called as small loaf of a *Nyasam* (knowledge). Actually, *Nyasam* on a particular subject is so vast to discuss or to explain. This is exactly why as a psychiatrist I am interested with few branches of Upanishath. In this way, I chose *Munduka Upanishath*.

After reading *Munduka Upanishath*, it gave me enormous insight for one reason, that to become wise, he has to transcend from the empirical world, which has the least knowledge on *Brahman*. This journey is said to be arduous. Hence, probably the individual's journey towards this path of ascendance would always call for a subject's pure submission to his own self in the form of *Niranhkara* (egoless). This is in principle opposite to what Pathanjali had taught in his *Kriya* Yoga, which talks on *Thapas* (austerity), *Swa Adhyaya* (self-learning) and *Eshwara Pranidhanaha* (submission to His abode). Yoga, according to Pathanjali, is man's pure submission to God. Whereas in Vedantha, to understand certain ancient dossiers, there should be an objective evidence (fitness) or a testament to his ability that whether he has submitted himself to his own ego or to his self. The objective evidence I could see here is *Muduka* or offering one's hair to his deity with piety. Let me not go into further description of mythological explanations to my present narration because it is endless (infinite), and arguments on such explanations would take us nowhere. In Hindu philosophy, a saint known to be filled with knowledge should not possess his hair (*Muduka*—shaving of his head). It has been explained that by offering one's hair in this way, the offered person would not be attracted or lured by any kind of *Vasana* (worldly attachments). It is all written in the scripture. Whatever theory I find in the scripture is for the *Pundit* to sort out, but what really I liked in this *Munduka* chapter is that this chapter of Upanishath had never asked obeisance, oblations and offerings to please the *Brahman* contrary to other chapters of Upanishath. This chapter explains only to know the *Brahman* to find a path towards being wise or *Moksha* (free from bondage). To explain it simpler, to know our *Ago Brahman* (universe), this script had never advised the pupil to offer material to fire (*Yagna*), it never had asked for the animal sacrifice nor it had ever asked the pupil to follow appeasement to God or unnecessary worships (rituals). Hence, the subject covered here is on knowledge and the knowledge alone.

I am not asking readers blindly follow whatever I have explained. My Open Meditation always preaches people to open their eyes before believing somebody or something and not believing someone just by closing their eyes. In other words, my Open Meditation would mean to be always aware and awake (*Jaagruth*). Invariably, we all feel that we are awake and conscious. There is every possibility that we are waylaid without our knowledge to be cheated or get ourselves mixed in some unusual problems. If we are not able to be wakeful, then there is every possibility that we tend to fall prey to the chaotic world, an example is our drowsiness while driving in the highway. My Open Meditation is a very simple technique to follow. This technique is like a mother answering to her just-born baby cries and answering to the babies' discomforts. Is this not amazing? A baby born from the *Suukshma Garbha* (mystic sanctum sanctorum) was answered immediately by the mother. The relevant example to my statement is the way by which a mother immediately enters to the baby's tiny consciousness. How could a mother explain this mix? Yes, it is simple; it is a mother and child relationship, an immense bondage. Similarly, the technique I teach on Open Meditation is simple. It has just three steps. First is to observe, second is to conceptualize and third is to reason. My technique of meditation is more useful for those who are habitually poor in their awareness (except in certain neurological pervasive disorders). My Open Meditation is not suitable for those who suffer from excessive daydreams. A mother never daydreams about her baby's needs, she is always vigilant and awake to manage her baby's needs. A simple baby cry is sufficient to make her more awake in spite of her awareness. When the baby is developing inside her womb, the mother had connected with her baby through the umbilical cord but not by her consciousness; hence, it is unspeakable that how fast she develops the true Yoga (mixing her consciousness with the baby's consciousness) with her baby. Many psychologists view that the developing foetus does invariably feel the pulse of its mother. The same story could be read from the epic story of Lord Krishna.

When Lord Krishna was inside his mother's womb, he was said to have listened to the stories told to his mother by many sages. What a revolutionary thinking in upbringing the infant if the aforesaid phenomenon is true because the foetus could be modulated towards positive psycho-social-physical health beforehand. At present, we have no prospective studies done to prove the mentioned modulation theory for good psychological well-being. If this technique rues the future, it is a boon to parents so as to design their children when born for "wants" and "don't want" in this world of reality. Assertively, the true spirit or the true awakening state that presently the men would require is for their good start-ups. Hence, I am of the opinion that my Open Meditation is one method that would increase physical, psychological and social well-being of many.

My Open Meditation technique also helps for those who daydream in spite of their full awareness. Frankly, I am against these dreams. Many laurels on this earth that have expressed their ultimate success is secondary to dreams, which they had experienced earlier. I have seen many men who had dreamt, later succumbing to their failures. They are left with despair, dejection and depression. The achievers express their dreams only after their achievements are met. Hence, success per se would come from their effort and approach and not out of their dreams. Hence, success is not accomplished by their dreams; success worked on their aspirations. Goals are different from aspirations. Aspiration is the fuel towards the goal to score. Messi never dreams while playing football. Before his free kick, if he dreams, he misses the goal. Hence, before a free kick, he has to have awareness on the distance from the spot he kicks to the goal post; he has to awaken the mathematics in his brain for a perfect curve to zoom past the goal post and the goalkeeper and he should ask his legs to act perfectly to kick for a goal. Aspirations are the basic force towards various goals. Aspiring is not bad, but having fixed goal is bad. Aspirations should be like water, which finds its own path. Aspirations are the developed inspirations in man to find his own destiny. Inspiration should not be pyrotechnics. Many inspirations lead to spoiled batter. Hence, inspiration should be limited inspiration and should try once. The beauty of the aspiration, the solace of achieving the aspiration and the contentment of the achiever makes a person famous.

Basically, the dreams are the metamorphosed pictures of self and the world. As a psychiatrist, I have seen many of my patients who had their wonderful dreams earlier and later same dreams disintegrating into vapours. To bring back their cherished dreams, I have to prescribe antidepressants to them. I am not a person who believes in pseudo-placards. The dreams and the goals are all right for "speech" of a speaker but never holds good in reality. Excessive daydreaming is a psychological morbid phenomenon observed in certain neurotic or psychotic disorders. The great Dutch, Vincent Van Gogh (1853–1890), was one who could put his daydream on a canvas sheet, but died harbouring psychosis.

There are few people who possess obsessions and compulsions, which are tormenting their self. These are the people who require psychiatric help. As such, man's de facto obsessions are a blessing in disguise. This obsession is necessary for our "striving" and not for our "brooding." This is a phenomenon that works inside our *Prajna* (consciousness), which we are not able to feel or express. Whatever could be the causes of this obsession, invariably, youth in this society are left with "irritability, anger and emotional outbursts." These are the people who require my Open Meditation because they are neither neurotics nor psychotics. Presently, youth require free flow technique to reach their destinations for ultimate cherishes. Hence, youth has to mix with the world of many "yes" or "no." After mixing too many opposites, he has to choose what is "yes" and what is "no." This is exactly what my Open Meditation tries to teach.

This chapter, *Munduka Upanishath,* which explains that "If a person observes, accepts and reasons the reality, he would find a path towards liberation (*Moksha*). An attempt to hold this path would make a person to be more aware, to be more attentive and to pay utmost concentration on the objects of his perception. The unwanted obsessions when snubbed or suppressed from the learnt knowledge of truth would allow a process of cognitive kindle to reduce the self-disturbances and consequent faulty expressions." This is exactly what the young and youth of this world would require, because all of them are swimming in this turbulent world. It is also said in some of the articles that the young, who has harboured obsessions of neurotic quality, when tries to mix with true friendship, it would reduce his obsessions and thus secondary depression. The art of mixing is called Open Meditation. By practicing this technique, it would enhance the deductive quality of a person. The deductive qualities are to subtract one's strong negative emotions or deduct many bad facets of a person while choosing a true friend.

Socrates said, "When a man who never explains or does not find logic to himself, then he is as good as dead." This statement of Socrates is exactly the same as that of Lord Buddha. He said, "As long as you keep fear, anxiety, guilt and despair, you are as good as dead." All these negative attributes are there with a man as long as he is not explainable to himself for many attributes that he would face or experience in his life. These attributes could be from his perceived issues, ideas or thoughts. These attributes could be from the problems or emotions that he could face. Hence, for a way to find the path towards being wise and to escape from the "Living dead" condition, a person has to learn three cognitive attributes. They are the three "A's" or otherwise "Aware, Accept and Act." "Aware" is to arouse one's self, "accept" is to arrive at an object or a subject and "act" is to activate one's consciousness. This technique a person could perform only when he is awake and by keeping his eyes wide open, not when he is obsessed, drowsy, sleepy or dull, except in certain psychiatric conditions. The reader could ponder on how my technique helps him. My technique is not big mechanics; the technique just requires a little attention and concentration to enter some bodies' mind, like husband to wife in her household works. An example is to sit by the side of her after her arduous work at home. For a worker to feel the pulse of his boss in procuring production, he decides to work a little more. The owner on seeing the promptness of his workers, he decides to reward them. A politician decides on granting governmental money for the basic infrastructure to his people, who elected him as their leader. Hence, for this type of small techniques, I christened it as Open Meditation.

I am amazed with *Munduka Upanishath* for this reason, as it says we are living with the knowledgeable reality (*Mithya*), though having highest knowledge that still lacks its perfectness. The absolute knowledge is always imperishable. Hence, it is beyond our knowledge, as this knowledge cannot be perceived totally. The knowledge the present *Brahman* has is beyond the seen (*Vyaktha*). I was reading an astronomy column about the multiple images of a supernova in a galaxy first seen. It really baffled the *Pundits,* but this phenomenon has been described earlier, I believe by Albert Einstein. Until now, the light ray has been thought to take a straight route, but in this phenomenon, the multiple images of the same supernova were due to the curved source of one light. The reason these astronomers have explained is that the light emitted from the supernova could have been influenced by the nearest black hole, which could have attracted the light rays emitted from the supernova, but passing rays would not have been completely absorbed by these black holes. Hence, same image to be multiplied depends on the strength of the innumerable galaxies or strong stars present by the side of the supernova and then the light emitted between them. It really baffled me, because customarily in our physics, we are taught that the light path is straight. This is exactly what the *Munduka Upanishath* explains, that there is nothing in this world by which we may know everything from our mere sacrifices to the God of fire, by worshiping the God or by our pure submission to the Lord's abode. We are going to know the whole thing in this world only by knowing from what is unknown. There is a saying that mankind dropped to this earth by the hypothetical God, where there was a process of knowledge too dropping from the highest to the lowest. There is a strong reason to believe in this statement because no anthropologist or evolutionist until now could substantiate that how trillions and trillions of hollow lives inside the human body could have weaved together and could function smoothly as one. Whatever we have till now are mere philosophical theories, but there is nothing in this world to prove these theories scientifically. In a similar fashion, if picture depictions on the walls of mythological great temples, where the aliens or the Gods would have descended on earth from interstellar space, who could have mated with primitive females and then subsequently could have genetically modified or engineered primordial genes to the present symmetrically shaped modern human beings of different colours and varied intelligence. After each moulding, beating and shaping of generational genes that could have taken place earlier, it probably culminated to groom wise *Manvantharas* or *Homo sapiens*. Out of many *Manvantharas*, Aristotle the great held the view of what was the purpose of life? After which, there was an attempt by the scholars to search their self-logic to find new reasons to transcend from the lowest to the highest. Hence, all great philosophers agreed to the point of argument that we humans would have possessed the philosophical attire to get their self-release from the shackles of bonded ignorance. In our earlier times, the philosophy was taught under metaphysics. In spite of all the philosophical explanations by philosophers, the monarch would have snubbed these philosophers and suppressed their views. Even though earlier earnest philosophers were executed systematically, and in spite of all these odds, till today, their views have found firm ground under the branch of psycholinguistic cognitive philosophies.

This is exactly what our *Vedantha* teaches today. If we go by the *Suthra*

Na Vedam Veda Ity Ahur Vede Vedo Na Vidyate.

Parathma Vedyate Yena Sa Vedo Veda Uchyate.

Verily, the *Veda* is not called to be *Veda* for there is no *Veda* in *Veda*. That is truly the *Veda* by which the Supreme is known.

I was disgusted to know that few modern leftist literary enthusiasts present today knew only to purge the *Anya Dharma* (different religions). As per their view, the *Dharma* that exists today is for only representing the two religions by two colours, green and white. God alone should forgive these literary buffs. I am happy that several literates turned their statements as the "way of living," *Dharma,* to which saffron stands for. I like those literates who are against the pseudo-religious people, who are exploiting monetarily on the ignorance and the innocence of the majority of men and women in our society. This attitude of ill elements in the society should be crushed and banned by the suitable law, as it is not good for few literates to blame the practices of a particular religion.

To explain the previously mentioned statement briefly, what we see in reality is perishable but to know the knowing of the *Brahman,* who is imperishable, we are not in a position to visualize him, hear him or sense him. The imperishable *Brahman* does not possess shelter, creed or cast. The imperishable also does not possess hands and legs. Hence, this imperishable is very subtle, omnipotent, omniscient and omnipresent. This is exactly the reason why this *Brahman* has been perceived as a "Being" or in Hindu mythology as Shiva. According to my understanding, I being a Brahmin, the goodness in me is Lord Shiva. Always, the "goodness" is all-pervading. Goodness does not expect, and is hence omnipresent. Goodness does not have any barrier, and is hence omniscient. Goodness has power to build the united world, and is hence omnipotent. The same theme has been explained in *Muduka Upanishath* as,

Yat Tad Adreshyam Agrahyam Agothram Avarnam Achaksho Sthrotham Tad Apani Padam.

Nithyam Vibhum Sarva Ghataam Sushyakshamaan Tad Avyayam Yad Bhuta Yonim Paripashyanthi Dhiraha.

There are many verses in *Munduka,* which are irrelevant to me, because being a psychiatrist I have focused on those verses that are relevant to my subject.

A verse in this *Munduka* kindled my brain, which is worth explaining here,

Yathorna Naabhihi Srujathe Grihyancha, Yatha Prithvivyam Osadhyayas Sambhavanthi.

Yathaha Santaha Purushath Kshelomani Tathaaksharaath Sambhavithaha Viswam.

Today, the Yoga has been distorted and has taken a corporate or business tag, because this Yoga has been restricted to only three parts, from eight limbs of true yoga. They are the "yoga *Asana*, *Prana Yama* and *Dhyaana*." The true Yoga says to "culminate." Hence, this Yoga always would mean to "mix" our mini conscious with mega *Brahman's* consciousness. For a reader, it is difficult to understand that how we could take our consciousness all the way to space and allow it to mix with the universal soul or consciousness. For this procedure, we need not hire any space aircrafts. This procedure also does not ask us to spend our precious time. This Yoga is a very easy procedure where we try to know the others' mind, which would bring the much-needed solace or probable happiness. In English, this procedure is called as Empathy. The same word in *Vedantha* is called as Yoga. A good psychiatrist, or for that matter any man with humbleness, would do the same with his clients or with other people, respectively. Empathy would mean going into the other person's shoes to find their feelings, whereas my Yoga or The Open Meditation is to go or mix with the others' consciousness to understand the logical events to their innumerable problems, which they could have come across in the present modern society. The process of going into the other person's shoes is not an arduous procedure if he is knowledgeable. For me to empathize with my clients, it has taken my degree and thirty years of my practice or psychiatric experience. Few fortunate people have this knowledge through their total submission to their self, like Mohan Das Karamchand Gandhi. My Open Meditation does not require any knowledge whatsoever, because this technique of mine would require just a bit of commonsense. Now, for example, in any given family of this competitive, colourful, interactive, informative and technological world, if I say a wife, by using her little commonsense, makes an effort to simply understand the husband's mind for reasons for coming late to the home, it would bring down automatically the divorce rate. I ask the reader to try this meditative technique in any given or perceived circumstance and also I ask the reader to experience the change he is going to have by way of mixing. For this, any person who has little patience after learning my Open Meditation would bring down the outbursts, bring down the unnecessary arguments, dilute the egoistic behavior and minimize the irritability. In my technique, there is no money or material transaction, it is a simple procedure to enter into some bodies' mind. The same procedure has been termed or used as metaphors, like in the movie *Precog*. Today, we are in the habit of using highly colourful terminologies for very simple words, example Mind talk for a counseling centre.

From this brief explanation, I would like to narrate the meaning for the above *Suthra,* which explains that how could imperishable be made to be understood by a man? It could be understood in the manner like a spider, which sends forth and draws its thread, as grass grows on the earth, as hair grows on our head and as the nail grow on our fingers. I am leaving apart the science part for these explanations, as they are difficult to understand subtly; similarly, understanding the imperishable part of the *Brahman* is also a difficult phenomenon.

Today's man, on contemplating mindfully, is grossly engrossed with three "M's," the material, money and muzzle. Hence, even though he could come out from this mess, it is true that he could presumably live with attachment, anger, hate, lust and despondency. This is exactly what Lord Buddha taught us as *Dukkha* or *Dummana* (sorrow). He had discovered a suitable method for the people to come out from *Dummana.* This discovery of his was *Sukha.* To get this *Sukha* (happiness), he had asked us to leave everything materially and mindfully behind. Under the present changing circumstances of the world, which is leaping forward algebraically, ambitious people have asked us not to follow what Buddha had taught. As Buddha was an enlightened master, he would have probably had the same previously mentioned logic three thousand years ago, and then, he could have arrived at the theory of ever-moving philosophy, as Dynamism. Hence, he had asked people to practice *Para Dharma* by their mind. The same teachings of his we now term as Compassion or Pure Love. This message one would achieve when we try the art of *Vipaasana* or the practice of *Mouna*. Off late, I have learnt that this *Mouna* could do wonders within the individuals psyche. Keeping this view, I am interested in explaining this *Suthra*.

Avidyaayaam Antare Vartamaanahaa Swayam Dheeraaha Panditham Manyamaanaha.

Yath Karmino Na Pariyanthi Muudaha Andhenaiva Niyamaana Yathaandhaah.

It is said that any wise individual should abide to some good principles in society. A person abiding in the midst of his ignorance would feel always that he is wise in his own esteem. He thinks that he is learned. He never feels that he is a fool. He also thinks that he does not get afflicted with troubles. He is so ignorant that he moves like a blind person even though he is not physically blind.

Avidyaayam Bahudaa Vartamaanaa Vayam Karthaarthaa Ity Abhimanyanthi Baalaaha.

Yat Karmino Na Pravedayanti Raagaath Tenaaturaah Kshinalokaaschvyavanthe.

The less knowledgeable person would live with many folds of ignorance. He would feel that he has accomplished everything under this world. Those who offer prayers and rituals would never try to understand the truth because of their innumerable attachments. Therefore, they sink to the bottom. Fruits of their merits by words and deeds would get exhausted or wretched in them if they do not come out of their ignorance.

Istaapuurtham Manyamaanana Vristam Naanyacha Kreyo Vedayanthe Prabuddhaah.

Naakasya Prasthe Ie Sukrutenubhutvemamm Lokam Hinanthraam Va Vishanthi.

Many deluded men feel that the practice of sacrifice to God is only the ultimate. They never feel that work is ultimate and important. Hence, they do not know any good. They forget that what we are enjoying today is heaven. This heaven could be enjoyed by a person only with his good deeds. If a man does not do good deeds in this world, he reaches to his lowest level.

Tapaha Shraddhe Ye Hy Upavasanty Aranye Santha Vidvaamso Bhaikshcharyaam Karanthaha.

Surya-Dvaarena Te Virajaaha Prayanthi Yatraa Mrutaha Sa Purusho Hy Avyayaathma.

When people practice austerity and faith in the forest, which is known for its tranquillity, one would attain a medicament to his mind or achieve the value of meditation as he gets freed from his sin or from the austerity that he performs in this atmosphere. This is what exactly a person who seeks would opt for or dwell into in the door steps of the Sun who is eternal, immortal and imperishable, and so will be called as real *Purusha.*

Many erstwhile *Vedhanthis* have explained religion in an elaborated manner. Religion is said to have arrived from the very roots of *Dharma.* Religion is based on rituals, customs and tradition. Whatever the facts on religion I have found, it is very baffling or confusing. I expect religion should be "one," free from the shackles of various rituals it could have possessed. Hence, I like the *Mudkuka* chapter, which is devoid of such rituals. According to me, rituals are compulsions. Compulsions are based on obsessions. Hence, man is riddled with fear, fear of life, death and God. To make my statement simpler, when our brain is full of obsession, where would be the space for outside knowledge to enter inside? True Yoga asks for some space in the mind to accommodate the knowledge to be learnt. As there are no spaces left, people never ever try to know the true nature of the world. For me, Religion is a fascinating word. I have a habit of dissecting the curious words like an anatomist who dissects a cadaver. When I dissect a particular word, I wonder about the meaning the word possesses. Today, religion is always emotional to people for the simple reason that it is nothing but "relay" in a "region." Whenever there is any trespass in a region of one *Dharma* to another *Dharma*, there would be a friction. Cumulated or collective frictions have led to divisions. This division is a decisive factor for the present social anarchy we are experiencing. Truly speaking, there is no immediate solution to the fire lit by us, it is burning our community. Different societies are being relocated and demarcated with religion, cast and creed. These demarcations are not by barbed wires but with deep scars in our souls. Hence, an instant soul search is required to extinguish the fire of hate, intimidation and impiety.

Coming to "relay" is like "relay race" in Olympics. Each participant country would try to win the race. Here, there would be an exchange of the baton whereas in "religion"; there are innumerable instruments, which are lineated from one sect to the same sect from generation to generations. Here, instead of baton, the genes, customs, traditions, rituals, etc. are exchanged. Hence, for a particular sect, their religion is too emotional. Because of this reason, nobody of any sect is likely to divulge, deviate and never ever likes to get interfered. In this situation, any trespass or cross-over would lead to mind or physical trauma in a person who ever ventures so. Simply, he would burn away physically or mentally.

In my consideration, "religion" is a misnomer. There should not be any religion because we are not justified to call ourselves as religious. Religion has no barriers or borders of its own. We created religion to our whims and fancies. Lord Buddha had no religion. His view on religion was to reduce the peoples' sorrow. He was a great discoverer, discovering the reasons for the sorrow." In his search, he could have acquired the enormous knowledge. After his lifetime study, he found a very simple reason for the peoples' "sorrow," and that he had named after the Sukha (happiness). Hence, religion should be restricted to only "knowledge." After years and years of knowing, probably he would have arrived to know a simple answer to the Hate. Yes, the answer he found was simple. It cannot be anything except Love. When this is done, I feel we could find a way to extinguish fire of "hate" on religious grounds. At the bottom of my arguments I had come to a compromising and comprehensive phrase and that phrase is "Religion is Good." Knowledge cannot be bad. When religion is knowledge, religion must be good too. When on the Law of land, only "good" prevails, then where would be the "fire?" Let our custom, tradition and rituals divulge but not the "feelings." This is exactly the hallmark of "human." Man has different religions but a human does not have any religion. A human is always humble with great humility. With all humility, a human is fully awake to perceive, fully accepts what he is going to perceive and fully reasons out what he had perceived about.

When knowledge is religion, why should different rituals exist in this world? *Munduka Upanishath* exactly teaches the same. As per the Upanishath, if a person submits himself to the knowledge and knowledge is alone the religion, what we speak should always be one. Lord Buddha did exactly the same. He had submitted himself to Compassion, Forgiveness and Love. Hence, the only ritual that existed for Lord Buddha was Mouna.

If we happen to go through various Upanishaths, the only explanation these Upanishaths render to us is to reach the bricks of the Alma Mater by our innumerable rituals performed, but contrary to all these Upanishaths, the *Munduka Upanishath* is the only exception, which says that it is not necessary to be religious or ritualistic to reach *Moksha* (ultimate abode to God). Further, it says that to be liberated there need not be any compulsions in offering of *Hawyaks* (scented sticks and grains) to God of Fire and also it is not our obligation to perform *Yagna*; it is our good deeds done that would always take us towards the path of *Moksha*. At this juncture, I would like to explain the meaning of Guru. In this sacred word, "*Gu*" would mean Guhya (cave) and "Ru" would mean Light in *Rigveda*. Hence, Guru is the one who brings light to the darkness or our ignorance. Here, it is for the seeker to kindle his senses by his learnt *Prathibha* (intelligence) to know his own *Anjana* (darkness). Intelligence is not a product manufactured inside our brain automatically.

Creator by default has endowed us with normal functions to perform, but He never gifted intelligence. The normal functions are just for our survival but intelligence has to be grabbed from outside to move forward, an example to have is 'luxury'. Probably He would have gifted art in a few. This art been gifted by creator to disperse the gifted art to his people around him. Fortunately or unfortunately, for few, this art is a commercial property. They are lucky to have such artist talent, but ninety-nine percent of people have to obtain intelligence from outside with great difficulty. Hence, a person who is interested in intelligence has to search and try to get it. While doing so, they come across many Gurus or moving fires in which darkness would melt away like butter. The most important period for the seeker is the space between moving fire of him towards the butter of understanding.

In Islam, following hunger rites during the period of Ramadan is for each brother to know what hunger means to the millions of people around the world. This is exactly the reason why they prefer to offer twenty percent of their earnings as offerings to people who are in need. This ritual is called *Zakaath*. This principal is followed all over the world with much fervour and piety. Since ages, these offerings have been applauded well all around the world. In *Munduka Upanishath,* there is a beautiful dossier for this which says:

Yasyaa Agnihothram Adarsham Apurna Maasam Achuthr-maasyam Anagrahyaanam Athithivarjitham Cha Ahutham Avaishwadevam Avidinaa Hutham Ye Sapthamasaha Tasya Loka Hinasthi.

The peasant who does obligation daily in his lands taking care of his family does not require any ritual to be performed to appease his God. He is the most liberated man. For a slightly liberated man, rituals of *Homa* and *Havana* does not constitute any basic necessity to reach *Moksha*. The farmer who has grown grains in that year, during his one-month period of his harvest time (the new moon to full moon), should invite his friends and relatives to share his grown grains and make them happy or otherwise the remaining months are said to be hell to this farmer. *Etesu* like this if farmer obliges to perform, his work, *Bhraajamaneshu,* is like a man possessing a great heart, his deeds are like *Suryasya Rasamaya,* sun's fruitful rays, and *Yaatra* is taken to *Devanam,* to that where the one Lord of the Gods is present.

The Goddess Kali (Chamundeshwari—possessor of sixteen hands and red tongue) is *Vishwa Rupan* (the mighty Goddess who owes responsibility to clean the world or to bring ills in the society to some order) and has been endowed with *Sapta Jivuha* (seven tongues of fire) to kill the *Karali,* the darkness, or *Anjana, Manojavaa* the bad or terrific, *Sulochitha,* the changing minds or the confusion, *Sudhumravarna,* the red or the people who are danger to the society, *Sphulangini,* the masked men and women who does appear like blitzing light threatening the harmony of the society, and *Leelaya Maanaaha,* like a humble servant using her moving tongue of fire to kill or destroy.

If a person who has learnt the art of destroying the evil just explained is received by Suryasya, the almighty Sun God, by throwing his arm of *Suvarna,* the gold, "Come, come dear friend," he is going to be termed as *Yajamana,* as Hero, and is welcomed with *Priya Vachana, Abhivadana,* with nice words, and honoured as *Aesha*; in this way, He the Lord welcomes him as *Brahman,* the knowledgeable.

After going through *Munduka Upanishath,* I arrived at a point that though reading this chapter did not answer my "belief" totally, certainly reading gave insight to my psycho spiritual science; hence, I believed the *Munduka Upanishath.*

In *Garuda Purana,* there is a beautiful dossier by our great Sage Vasista, who had addressed Lord Rama as,

Kaalam Yajna-Tapo-Dhana-Theertha-Devaarchana-Brahma
Chiram Aadi, Satopetaha Kshapyanthi Mruga Iva.

"Look, by doing mere sacrifice, austerity, alms giving and pilgrimage with worshiping God would allow you only to reach nowhere and would produce mere misery to you. You are not human any more but you are a beast, remember." This mighty Sage would not end there and he goes further by saying "Those who work for their own Caste and Religion were devoid of their Values and Virtues. Hence, they ruin their own pride."

There is another interesting verse in *Garuda Purana,* which I would like to mention,

Eka Bhooka Tho Paavasha Aadyair Niyamaha Kaaya
Shoshanaiah Mudhaha Parokshам Icchaanthi Mama Maya
Vimohithiha.

Today, there is a passion that prevails with people, because of which, in some auspicious days, some ritualistic men and women perform fasting. Generally, people are very concerned of their own body. To explain briefly, our body is a super big chemical factory in which organic and inorganic elements keep on exchanging themselves for our physical and mental well-being. Without this chemical permutations and combination inside our body, practically we are dead. The chemicals abide to their own Law of Nature to execute their own specific functions at specific time synthesizing life-saving chemicals during our wee hours of stress every day to bring back the required homeostasis. All these chemical reactions would take place in each individual living cells, which are more intelligent than us. When compared to living beings, trillions of trillions cells inside us are self-satisfied, more friendly and never intrude to other cell's territory. All these cells work together relentlessly for a remedy. This factory needs raw materials like food from an outside source and electricity, which generates by self in our Reticular Activating System of brain and from our Auricular Node situated in our heart. Deficit raw material would lead to hunger and alter the chemical functions inside our body. The low glucose level leads to abnormal functions of brain. Cells do not know food has to be purchased but cells need not purchase the oxygen, as it is abundantly available outside. Therefore, invariably the Mind and the body works together in this amazing world of living species towards peace and health.

A limited intake of food or partial starvation existed with people since ages on certain afflictions and on certain diseases to give rest to the mind and body. Now this has become a new trend with religious people, like in *Ekadashi*, *Dwaadeshi* or on few festivals, when Hindu religious people practice partial starvation. This starvation is also a disease in certain OCD's (Obsessive Compulsive Disorder) like in Anorexia Nervosa, in which the individual starve to remain thin. Partial starving could be customary practices with certain religious sects. Jain community practices forced starvation to reach the Lord's abode when they are aged. This practice amounts to euthanasia. Hence, this customary practice has led to many legal battles in our country to practice or not to practice. Fine, it is good that people starve so that peoples' endocrinal system would come under some check. My contention is that, or that of the above-said verses, when we are keeping all ill in people's mind, why should people clean their bodies in the name of purification? The true purification should take place in the mind, not in the body. A single meal would make a person weak. I explain my experiences further.

In our Hindu customs, we follow *Shraaddha* (submission) ritual to please the ancestral departed souls, and also by performing these rituals, it is proclaimed that we are able to direct their souls to reach the God's abode. After my father's death, I performed this ritual. This ritual is done with all fear and sanctity. Oblivious to this ritual, a lot of sacrifice had to be done to Brahmins. Obviously, these rituals invariably incur lots of money. These rituals also consume lots of time. The meanings to every stage of these rituals are truly fantastic and the fact is that we perform this ritual by knowing that the departed soul never comes back. I did this ritual. Frankly, I will ask my son not to do this because I am not worthy to send my soul to heaven. I cannot testify if he will do this ritual or not. After performing this ritual, it had happened that before we eat a grand lunch on this auspicious day, we have to offer the imagined souls (solid batter) of my father, grandfather and fore grandfather to crows or to fish or to cows. I was asked to fast in the morning. To tell frankly, I had starved, my glucose levels were down, my cognition was impaired; there was no *Shraddha* in my *Shraddha* ritual. My reflexes were low; I took my brother-in-law's four-wheeler to offer the three *Pindas* (imaginary invoked *Athmas*) to fish in a pond. Austerity in performing the ritual would be required by the performer. Actually speaking, it was not there in me because I had starved. To explain, my Judgment was impaired even in calculating the distance of a two-wheeler coming behind me, through the rear mirror. Judging a vehicle in the rear mirror appears far off though it is near.

I took a right turn without looking or observing by turning head due to my low reflexes and impaired cognition in my mind. The bike had collided straight in the middle of my vehicle perpendicularly. The accident was not serious but it left cuts and bruises to the pillion rider and fracture of the clavicle to the rider. If I had taken breakfast on this day, the accident could have been prevented. There are so many stories of this kind wherein people have lost their lives offering *Pinda* (solid batter prepared by mixing honey, banana, milk, and rice powder with wheat powder, with shaping or moulding the solid batter in the form of imaginary human with head, trunk and legs). My sincere advice to the readers is that people should not forget to do these rituals, as it has various hidden meanings but they should perform the same not without a full stomach.

This story would throw a light on how our body functions. With inefficient or deficient chemicals, our body disorganizes itself to function abnormally, hence, imagine how important hunger would be. In some of the poorest of poor nations, people die like insects due to internal social anarchy riddled with civil wars that have allowed these nations to be torn apart not by mere bloodshed but because of their starvation. Hence, religion would speak to its mouth by relaying (supply) the food to the poorest of the poor. To offer food or helping the poor is not restricted to any cast, sect or religion. Therefore, any individual having humility to address the pulse of any needy population in this world is religious. Hence, even poor could be religious. In our country, individuals paying prompt income tax are religious. It does not matter to the individual as to which community he came from. This is why I term religion as "One" or universal. Hence, presently the existence of religion is at jeopardy. According to Pluto, "We are ignorant at all quarters. We make headway to a cave. We lit a fire behind us and there is a wall in front. We are fools as we realize our own images as real. When we find no fruits, exposing to sun tells us all the truth." Religion and God's are actually objective realities and also are our mere notions.

The preachers all over the world belonging to innumerable sects rooted deeply the religion into individuals for a diversified stalemate. The religion is not by the Gods, but religion created by us. If our mythology is correct or if we believe extra-terrestrial existence, then by all probability, Gods are the ones who did all the impossible to mankind by building unimaginable archaeological marvels in this world belonging to all faith, to all religion and to all sects of people. This is why I reassert that "Religion" is the blue print of "Oneness." Hence, when GOD is one, we all should practice our religion as one religion, religion of Humanity. This day is not far; one day we all would see and feel ourselves as one "*Homo sapiens*" to fight against the Robots.

ROBOTS

There is little difference between Bhagvad Geetha to *Ashta Vakra Geetha.* To my knowledge, both would impart the same virtues to a new reader by measurement. Though both epic stories are the same type of movies, the settings and the shooting of the two movies are at different locations. In Bhagvad Geetha, Lord Krishna gave the necessary medicine to Arjuna for succouring *Dharma.* In *Ashta Vakra Geetha,* Saint Ashta Vakra relieved the delusions of Janaka Maharaja who had harboured ignorance. Both *Geethas* stood on *Karma* (action). This *Karma* I have already explained in depth in my first English book Parivarthana (the change). To explain briefly about this *Karma*, it is not just a blind faith or blame on to the *Vidhi* (bad moment). This *Karma* is neither an Action nor Causal to the contemporary preachings of present *Vedantha.* The causation and actions are limited to a particular context or situation. This could be either psychological or physical. This equation equals physics Law of Motion equation, which has been explained as "For every action there is an equal reaction." Hence, physics *Karma* is very much restricted. So, the *Karma* what I narrate is beyond what physics says. According to me, this *Karma* is a dynamic force towards liberation and celebrations than to mere restrictions. This world or the *Brahman* is a cheat because He does not want *Samsara* (life as per Lord Buddha) to end. The purpose of man's survival depends on *Brahman's* survival. This Universe always thrives for its existence. Hence, He would not allow man to be liberated, so He celebrates. When man is liberated completely, there ends the human rein or the end of the world. This is to convey that if man does not exist in this world, then the world ceases. The present Robots manufactured could recognize and dwell with us but by no chance are these Robots able to communicate with Nature or with the *Brahman*. Hence, tomorrows *Karma* as per law of Physics is stationary than dynamic. When these manufactured Robots loose the very purpose to propagate their species to know and understand this *Brahman* and also they are not able to live with the *Brahman* effectively then the very nectar of *Karma* is lost and Natural ambrosia gets putrefied. The path of *Karma's* purification is not going to stop in one generation. This purification would require several generations. The "gene" or the "seed of *Karma*" would keep on refining to the point of *Jeevana Mukthi* as long as this *Brahman* is going to stay. If this *Brahman* remains eternally, the very essence of consciousness (awareness, analysis and reasoning) of human should also remain too. I am sure that these Robots manufactured would not house the type of consciousness I have previously mentioned. There is a reason to say this. I had read a story where a great wrestler was about to fight, and stopped fighting with his opponent because his opponent spat on his face before the scheduled match. This wrestler was sure of his defeat against his opponent as he would harbour "anger." By explaining this analogy, I have a doubt whether the future manufactured Robots would be able to emulate the same reasoning and analysing capacity?

Fine, I may not be alive to feel and see fifty years ahead from this day, but coming back to my *Karma,* I have something to make a statement. When I have committed or pronounced that the *Karma* is "Gene," one should not get obsessed literally, because this hypothesis of mine would draw controversy. It is like talking against God. I am a moderate rationalist who sees many spiritual phrases in a science perspective. To embark on to my statements, I do not possess any modern labs to testify scientifically. It is my visionary of my experience and learning to make much of my statements on a fictious note. Many past fictions have become reality now. In this moment, I am drawing mere conjectural assessments rather than solid or concrete object-related answers. Once again, about *Karma* or the "gene" theory, I am of the possible opinion that mere application of good and bad attitudes or characters by a particular race would have a tremendous impact for further generations of the same race to upgrade or degrade their own generational progenies. This is how exactly our modified, well-evolved Forebrain had developed from ancestral *Homo erectus* to present *Homo sapiens.* As per evolutionists, this process would have taken approximately millions of years. Hence, at this juncture I am interested in something called "missing link."

MISSING LINK

Truly speaking, I am unable to relate a link between the amazingly evolved present social animal or today's analytical man from the prehistoric reptiles as all evolutionist books try to explain. Today, we are endowed with great softwares to fuse our looks to prehistoric reptiles. As days and years passed from Stone Age to Neolithic Age, the then useless organs have converted into the functionless present rudimentary organs. Biologists now proclaim that these organs as useless rudimentary organs, which could be removed without much fuss. Hence, some popular surgeons made their fortunes from these rudiments like tonsils and appendix. Archaeologists of the present era kept exploring undiscovered places on this earth to find different mummies and fossils of Prehistoric or Stone Age or Medieval human bones for a missing link. I had read an article that archaeologists have discovered a part of a finger bone dating back to hundred million years. By these discoveries, present-day evolutionists and anthropologists are on their toes to unravel the mysteries behind such bones and try to link or explain logic towards the development of reasoning brain like ours. There are many movies depicting the discovery of elongated skulls with all details of present skull except the voluminous room for the forebrain that could have accommodated then brain. If this theory is true, the prehistoric *Homo sapiens* were more intelligent when compared to present humans. I am of the opinion that with such elongated skull, they could have possessed elongated occipital fusiform lobe. This form of skull they would have possessed for their depth on future psychological vision. Today, we are modified and we do not see such a type of skull for the simple reason that we are too narrow minded and are having shallow vision. This statement exactly fits into the reductionist view of evolution. Millions of years ago, ancestors were said to be tall, and today, we are living short in all quarters, including our thinking. One possible reason for our narrow thinking could be due to the pathetic approach towards the evolving philosophy. This philosophical development has made man mean by continuous onslaught on healthy philosophy from non-healthy argumentations and also by reductive views on philosophy by reductionists. The paradox is that instead of getting more refined in our thinking, we have changed to evildoers. Because of this negative mental path, we are growing shorter and thinking narrower.

Coming back to the point of missing link, what have we missed? According to me, we have missed a beautiful strong crocodile's tail. In this analogy, crocodile has missed a wonderful brain like ours. This is what I say "Missing Link." This is my pure observation and the narration that what I am going to narrate is my own. Prehistorically, the huge crocodiles were roaming freely on this earth. Millions of years have passed since then, but except for a small change in the form of its shape and their stunted growth, these crocodiles remain same as they are. The man is the opposite of these creatures wherein he has evolved himself from "Nil" forebrain to "Full" forebrain. How would one think of this mystique transformation? For this dilemma, as per my view, probably there is a missing link between

"Crocodiles" and "Man" for one simple reason that we are yet to discover "Croco–humanoid" creatures. Till now, I have no idea of such creatures' existence. However, this previously mentioned mystic animal, if at all we find, would not miss a link and that link would be the "Ferocity." A crocodile is ferocious by its look so also the same is true with man; not by his looks, but by his ferocious mind. The whole world lives in fiction, so also its members are fictitious. Therefore, I am not different when I conjure on fiction and doubts on fictitious attitude from my fellow humans. In a fictional scene, I love to visualize half man and half animal. If this croco– humanoid existence were to be true as some mythological figures, pictograms, fossils and portraits available on such animals, I am hundred percent sure that we have not missed any link from our ancestral Amoeba to Humans. Today, in our technology, like social media, some messaged images of half human, half fish and half birds flying is circulating freely all over the world. I am not a professor to ascertain these images but rather I am sceptical about the authenticity of these images. I think that these images could have been morphed in the social media. The movies on fiction or thriller always would allow persons more pleasurable to watch. In this way, for me, imagining creatures of multiple animo–humanoids mystifies me. Imagine a life with fish fins, crocodile tail, horse legs, chimpanzee's trunk and human head. In this lineage animal, nowhere is the link missed. Can anybody say what had happened to these lives? As and when man got evolved, if the evolution theory is correct, the fish automatically should disappear or get extinct? How could we answer that fish is fish, crocodile is crocodile, horse is horse, chimpanzee is chimpanzee and man is man today? If this statement of mine is a reality, then what is evolution? Where are the mythological animo–humanoids? My contention is that if Charles Darwin's evolutional theory is true, then in this vast Universe, we should have found mixed animals or mixed humans. By with all practicality, let us assume that these mixed lives would have lived happily and peacefully millions of years ago. If this statement of mine is true, then what had happened to them? Did they disappear on earth during the ice age or by asteroid collision? Or, did they get extinct by some viral or bacterial infections? Hence I would think that these animo–humanoids were killed and destroyed from this earth by mean minded man due to his "Fear," which he had possessed for his own survival. Man could not have killed all these mystical or mythological lives without his hands. Forebrain and the hands are the greatest assets of *Homo erectus* and *Homo sepia.* Ancestors could have used the sharp instruments invented and also from their evolved forebrain they could have sketched to go on a rampage or could have gone on killing spree of the aforesaid mystic animals. This marauding behavior of our ancestors would have wiped out the different mixed races from our land thousands of years ago. This could be a probable theory from, which we are surviving even today at the expense of these mysterious mixed animals or half humans roaming freely earlier.

Mayans, Greeks, Egyptians, and Hindu mythological temples were said to have been built by the then monarchs and ancient aliens. These aliens would have landed long ago and helped them in constructing these monuments. To make this more interesting, the old pictures of aliens carved on the walls have been discovered across many huge and amazing temples, which are impossible to imagine or impossible to construct such architect marvels. The constructions of such structures are possible by only Gods not by men. Who are they? If we go into the depth of those authors who worked relentlessly travelling and understanding such great structures, I am of the view that millions of years ago there was a link between cosmos and the prehistoric *Homo sapiens*. How could they land, on whose invitation they came to this earth? On all these temples or structures, an enthusiast finds iconography carved on stones and wood where Kings invited these powerful ancient aliens or virulent Gods through their human sacrifices and appeasing them with blood. Probably our blood, which has protein intervened with genes, could have missile energy to cosmos and in turn Gods would have decoded the invitation and arrived on earth. I have mentioned virulent Gods, which meant male Gods, not female Gods. What does this statement mean? Primordial humans of this era would have allowed these Gods to mate with Neanderthal women. Hence, such oblique skulls are the product of Gods and our ancestral women. The link what I have missed here is the duration of these Gods stay, and the life of these productive offsprings who had really survived. What made our skull symmetrically round and heart shaped? God only knows. Evolutionists have answers for this logic by theory of redundancy or by theory of adaptation or by theory of survival of the fittest from millions of years. The symmetry what I have mentioned could be due to the charged inorganic matter of earth's gravitational force. To answer all these links that are missed or not missed, probably the deep study of human genes by mega mapping and through thorough decoding would throw a possible answer for my link someday by our scientists.

In our Hindu Mythology, what I have just mentioned, the half animal and half human, has been discussed under *Dasha Avathara's* (ten reincarnations). The transformation or metamorphosis through reincarnation of the Lord Vishnu, the creator, mover and caretaker, are all well documented and explained in the ancient Puranas (from *Mathsya*—fish to *Kalki*—man the mean). Deep understanding of the body experience, extra-terrestrial phenomenon, unidentified floating objects and the Gods or aliens would likely throw a light on our knowledge. In my practice, while taking history, I enquire patients regarding their dreams, and those invariably depressed (neurotic depressions) explain snake in their dreams. I feel happy when I listen to them because at least here I have not missed any link between man and reptiles.

COGNITION

Cognition is the foremost function of the brain. Leaving thoughts, action, will and feelings apart, all other functions come under this domain, to be precise. Will is a philosophical state having a *Vedanthic* touch and action is more of *Karma* or the business part of life. For me, "Cognized that which is perception and this perception is associated with emotion is cognition." If we consider the word "Cognitive" and divide the same on a hypothetical divisionary technique, what derives is "Ignition of the consciousness combining with neither confidence nor no confidence." Hence, in a sense the *Prathibha* (inner light) of an individual, which throws its light on various functions of brain to execute combined activity having invariably a clean path in general, could be called as "Cognition." This cognition, *Suva Moto,* is waste if will and action are not called upon by the mind for the simple reason that will is like a thrust in a machine and action is its forward momentum. In-between this thrust and momentum, what we do not see is cognition. Therefore, for the *Purusha* this *Maya* or the illusionary world is an impetus for the body to act. Hence, as long as the world exists, our actions could be observed in this fictional world or object reality, mind tends to become more fictitious. Hence, this is more of an infection. Leaving apart social networking, where tweeting and blogs go viral, we have another mode of illusionary e-virus of virtual images; giving a lecture in one place can be beamed through live holograms in all dimensions at various places across the world simultaneously. Is this not technological infection?

The brain has millions and trillions of neurons associated with lakhs and lakhs of inter-connecting centres just like our universe with stellar constellations having millions and billions of stars and planets in each one of such constellations. How the universe united and allowed each planet and star to function by finding its own path is still unanswered. Unbelievably, the mammoth Lord Bhairava (infinite universe) was magnanimous enough to impart neutron and proton in our life for us to experience Him. The processes of fitting these micro-lives into our organic case by the creator have taken millions and millions of years. Let us not bring to mind an evolutionist and as well as a philosopher, who are always obsessed about our evolvement and our intelligence. Have we ever asked ourselves, "What is the purpose of my life in this earth?" There are innumerable illustrations and individual narrations on this topic to the whims and fancies of the explainer. I also would try to explain the same in my own way. While having a chat with one of my friend, who is an anaesthetist, after my ECT (Electro Convulsive Treatment) session at six o'clock early in the morning regarding a brachial nerve block, which he had given to a patient just three hours earlier to correct the fracture in the lower part of humorous bone, I was curious to know the procedure of this block, which he had tried. Today surgical as well as anaesthetic fields have changed a lot for the benefit of patients in terms of minimal invasive bloodless surgeries and short stay in the hospitals because doctors are costly and hospitals have become more expensive.

He was narrating the art of passing and manoeuvring the needle in the arm to block the brachial nerve to operate upon fractured bone humorous. I was surprised to hear his guiding narrations in principle towards an unseen place. The explanation narrated by him was such that he is already near to the nerve, which is tending to be blocked. Form this story, it is clear that the very purpose of our life is to acquire the knowledge, to impart the good and pass on the benefits. This is exactly what my Open Meditation would mean. This technique could not have been done by meditation with closed eyes because an anaesthetist has to feel and see the landmarks to pierce and manoeuvre the needle by tilting the arm to certain angles before he could hit the bull's eye. In our subtle life environment, we need to learn or know all these guiding and manoeuvring techniques to place oneself in another person's shoes to perceive their right thoughts and feelings to live and let live. We cannot do these manoeuvres by not observing somebody's expressions. Hence, in our life, we all should open our eyes to interact without hurting. Frequent psycho-social bumps with our closed eyes could lead to non-lasting mental agonies.

The definition of my Open Meditation is "It is a state of one's journey, in which when a man while awake takes his awaken state to subtle inner state, repair his own conflicts, confusions and contradictions for a reasonable remedy." Hence, Open Meditation is a simple procedural technique done individually in a state of awaken state to douse off the fires that could light up everyday's life out of our unwanted frictions. My Open Meditation is something that never talks on energy, aura, power, vibration, magnetism, black magic, *Kundalini*, astrology and also about Gods; my technique simply asks the subject to conjure on his object for a change in him, and to experience the relief from the stress he was in. He could experience the said magic by way of "Mixing," a Yogic word, "Intelligence," an English word, "Subtle," a *Vedanthic* word, and "Meditation" a Spiritual word with a perceivable object. My Open Meditation is a technique, in which knowledge or experiences have no known roles to play. My Open Meditation does not ask for any special space or a particular time My Open Meditative practice could be done anywhere and at any time or on a particular moment. This technique teaches to sail smooth or like a driver driving a car smoothly, with no unnecessary jerks and no unusual brakes. Jerks would be fearful, with fear of foreseeable future, anxiety, anticipating non-performance, despondency and thinking the world be bleak. Breaks would be inattentiveness, poor concentration, losing temper, irritability, no patience, not adjusting, etc. For a smooth drive, the driver has to be more watch full to enjoy the car ride. No grunting, no remarks, no abuses and no expressions, it is all smooth sailing by the driver, as he makes his drive smooth. If we practice this dictum, I am sure there would be no Road Razes ("Raze or razor" is a concept on road raze in my first book Parivarthana—the change). The practice of this Open Meditation could be a chapter to anyone if he has the deep understanding to himself, relating well to this world, has found the pulse of different worldly lives, knows the roots of his customs, culture and tradition and finally he has to have tolerance to the different religions. The awaking watchfulness, happy wakeful listening, good amount of analysing with reasoning and heartfelt smiles are the prerequisites for my Open Meditation. This technique is like Sigmund Freud's free association. In "Free association," the patient freely associates in his thoughts with the treating psychiatrist, whereas in my technique, each individual freely has access to the minds of fellow beings. This Open Meditation technique is not a precognition or premonition of terrible and mystic things that happen in life. My technique is to freely sail across the world of psycho-social turbulences, so as to bring back the mind and body into some order. Finally, mind remedy is the cliché of the day.

CRICKET, THE TICKET FOR TRANSFORMATION

Weekend is a bane for many of us, unless we have forcibly tuned ourselves to watch TV with the usual soaps (soap irritates the eyes) and reverberating News (chewing gums) or have a habit of reading the central page editorials in our Sunday newspapers. I do not act differently on a Sunday, as I could not concentrate on watching or reading; hence, I decided to take a walk on a busy road to find any interesting fests or dramas in my town. To my bad luck, there were no interesting programs in the city Town Hall and also in *Sahithya Bhavan* (literary building), except dust irritating my nostrils and poisoning my lungs to a little extent from the CO (carbon monoxide)emission by passing vehicles. I knew about this, but still I cannot escape from walking, as my town roads are heavily congested to try to go by car. I wanted to play safe when my health is concerned; hence, I decided to walk cross roads and conservancies to get free from these hazardous pollutions. It is unfortunate to observe that all conservancy cross roads are cemented, thus preventing recharge of my town bore wells by rainwater. It is the destiny of a taxpayer to suffer because of the disillusioned governmental works. Fine, I have to move on and live on in spite of all the trouble as I have been born in this God-given country. I had met one of the retired professors in English who had advised me to write a book on "personality development." This happened when I had been to him requesting a forward note for my first English book, "Bend and Mend." Keeping the same thought in my mind, I went inside a book stall to find such books. While searching for such books, I found several that talked about the new *Avathars* to tame and tune the minds of adolescents. To my available time, I glanced through some of the books on personality development written by "Personality Guru's." To my astonishment, I found these books with hundred and fifty to two hundred pages, quoting philosophers' views with psychological jugglery of words, which one could find in psychiatry and philosophy textbooks. Simple punctuations, verbs and adjectives were missing, and actually, for me, being a practicing psychiatrist, the contents in these books were difficult for me to format in my brain. I felt that in the rack there were many books on psychology with original works of great psychologists, which were interesting to postgraduate students of psychology; similarly, many such books on management, skill development and on corporate views are of interest to MBA graduates. I was really confused to know the mind of an honest adolescent, making his or her new strides in education or business, and when he tries to read such books it would invariably lead to chaos in his brain, which might hamper the further acquisition of extra knowledge in him. This is my observation in my practice, that if a student with interest tries to read such books, he might not understand completely what is written in these books, or when he tries to know the contents, it would lead to obsession in him, thus leading to scholastic downfall. My sincere advice for the young is to listen to their teachers who have mastered such skills. Hence, these books should be read as a hobby and not to pursue in their casual studies. Spending one hour in a bookstall is like gazing at the stars. With hurry burry, I kindled my feet to back out from the bookstall, with no choice other than polluted atmosphere and bad roads to find my way back home.

On my way back to home, to prevent my lungs from CO (carbon monoxide), I took a short route bisecting my town municipal grounds. When I began my practice, in 1984, this ground was amazingly filled with enthusiastic young players and was heaven for many elderly to burn their calories. This ground originally had spread across fifteen to twenty acres and was shaped rectangular. That was the time I played cricket. I found speeding a leather ball curtailed my reflexes while batting, which sullen the game of my leather ball cricket, except for playing occasionally tennis ball cricket to flatten my bulging belly. Slowly, I switched over to tennis and badminton from the game of cricket. It is a sorry state of affairs to see, today, that such a huge magnanimous playground is occupied by a newly built hospital on the southwest of the ground, which has engulfed more than one-quarter of the earlier playground. Meanwhile, for this upcoming hospital building, the old institutes, like pre university college, and a reasonable part of girl's high school were demolished to accommodate. The church, not demolished by the side, is still standing tall as a testimony to the tricks practiced by a local politician's minority appeasing techniques. Fine, we all should love every religion for the better progress of our country, but I hate politician's political gain. If we observe this playground now, it is being kept in shambles, with garbage lit all over and plastic covers strewn on every corner. In my first book, "Parivarthana (the change)" I have written in detail regarding importance of such playgrounds. Playgrounds are epicentres for the youth to discharge their energy and for their obsessive free reading by engaging in different games in the playgrounds, which are available to them. It was evening when I stepped in this half-distorted playground from the west side. This was a beautiful scene with the sun dawning, emitting red light with a hew laser colour lighting the whole stadium to an illusionary fictitious scene. It was nice to hear prayers from the nearby mosque, church bell ringing and chanting Vedic *Manthras* from a distant temple. Because of the constricted space, restrained young players, aged fifteen to twenty-five years, irrespective of their religion, were playing cricket in the pitch placed north–south. Earlier, I remember there were probably six to eight pitches in rows with fifteen to twenty players in each team. Now teams were constrained to two to three. Watching the existing college wall as wickets, it was nostalgia of my young cricketing days. As there was no place behind the bowler, I had to walk between the bowler and the batsman for fear of my head being hit with the tennis ball. When I had observed these young players in groups, half were Urdu-speaking players of the west and half were Kannada-speaking teams playing of the east; I felt grieved, as young boys were divided on language we speak and the religion we follow. Nothing to worry, still all is good because after all it is the spirit of play that matters more. It was an amazing scene to me to observe the ball being thrown, ball being hit, players juggling around to catch the ball, captain yelling at his fellow players, captain abusing the underperforming players and picking quarrels on simple issues, each player does not let his ego down. It was still amazing to watch elders in ten or twelve in numbers discussing national and local issues on a flag-hoisting platform in the northern part of the playground. As the Urdu-speaking boys outnumbered Kannada-speaking players, my brain ignited regarding a ticket to cricket for the young boys who are prone to glue (adhesives and other solvents) sniffing. This habit of solvent inhalation has spread like viral disease in some of the communities who are under-privileged and downtrodden. This habit also has been seen with young boys who work in the workshops and the garages. Probably, I might be right that some of these boys were playing cricket to get away from their addiction or from the substances they use. We have to encourage such young boys to play cricket to get free from their solvent sniffing, which is a dangerous habit and these solvents are cheap and easy to obtain. When the readers find such young boys sniffing, they should encourage them to play the game of cricket for their transformations (free from addiction). Let us pray for the playgrounds to remain as they are from the encroachers for our good future. I was walking alone a three to four kilometres stretch during which time no one recognized me and I desired in one corner of my mind to be recognized. Finally, from my heart, I did not want to be recognized. (I have narrated a concept Actor on people's recognition with antecedent problems in my English book Parivarthana—the change).

EXPERIENCE, EXPERIMENT AND EXPECTATIONS

Doctor, I had a message in WhatsApp recently, which had read "yesterday's experience, today's experiment and tomorrow's expectations," and the message says further, "To use our experiences by the experiments to achieve our greater expectations." I am confused doctor. Could you explain?

Very interesting, all these three words have "Ex." Anyway, how is your "Ex"-wife.

"No contact, Dr"

How can you have contact with your wife when you are married to your WhatsApp? Today's young generation, irrespective of their sex, cast and religion have one thing in common, the "technology." Today, the world of technology is like two edges of a sharp dagger. The safest edge of the dagger is a wooden handle. To kill or to escape from getting killed, a person should hold this wooden handle tight. Many people hypothetically consider that the man who always presumed to be safe should hold daggers by the wooden handle only. However, this thinking is wrong. If the above statement is right today, then why the safe part of the man's world is suffocating and squeezed from the ever-growing technology and competition? Carefully, you all think on my explanation. Good life and peaceful life are totally different. All good people need not have peace in their mind. Good life is materialistic life compared to peaceful life, which is spiritual in nature. Good life is more objective in a realistic world whereas peaceful life is more of a subjective in our conscious world. It is said that peaceful life is a prerogative to good life. Today, we are going to have smart cities, which probably provide good life, but I doubt about the peaceful life. In this technological world, the peaceful life is inversely proportional to good life. Good life we are talking today is on outside infrastructure but not by any inside psycho spiritual paths. I am there in a smart city but away from true spirituality. Hence, I struck to or reassert to "splendour city" than a smart city. Smart cities are for corporate people. Splendour city is for the humble humans. This is exactly what I regard to safeness about holding a knife with its wooden handle, which is not always safe. We always should think while holding a dagger that the sharp part of the knife is near to our hand. Any time knowingly or unknowingly, dagger can cut our fingers, because we are not able to hold the safe wooden handle always tight. To be peaceful in this growing technological world, one should expect the worst. Hence, to overcome the worst, one would play the safeness in bringing back the peace. There is a tendency for a man to lose his grip due to ever-growing technology, which paves way for his inattention and lack of concentration. While holding the knife, if "Peace" is wooden handle, two edges are the "Development" and "Technology." According to me, these two never go hand-in-hand. Development ruins the inner peace and technology brings the competition. When development doubles and technology triples, knifes with wooden handle would burn and crack. Hence, simple holding of this dagger leads to a deep cut. Therefore, in these circumstances, man has to hold on to the blade of the knife not the edges of this knife. Hence, here what you require is the art of holding the blade, which has sharp edges of a knife, the "Development" and the "Technology." Such holding should not bring a cut in your finger. This is possible by three "P's," they are perception, patience and punctuality. Whatever I am explaining to you is not for any argument. My explanations are for our understanding. I am talking about the myths of smartness and development. This is exactly what I would like to assert about "Development" and "Technology," both never bring "Peace." Yes, peace is a possibility in this world when we are able to understand, reason out and analyze properly the technology and the subsequent development. In today's world, we all probably think world is good and safe but the competition part of the same world probably destroys the ethos of the society and morality of its people.

Hence, as per my statement, I would like to convey to you that keeping dagger in your home is not safe at all. Therefore, the present hype on our development is actually like a dagger. I do not say that we should live in the dark, but the development should parallel with wellness of any society. This well-being could be mental, physical or social. According to the World Health Organisation, even spirituality has been included in defining health. Well, this spiritualism, which has been included in WHO is not my teaching of spiritualism. My spiritualism is Open spirituality, not occult spirituality. To be brief, once again my spiritualism is the study of the high feeling experienced by humans without consumption of spirit (alcohol), consuming alcohol is said to induce high feeling.

Now you understand how dagger is dangerous. Mere thinking of dagger, possessing of dagger or using dagger as weapon, all these ideas would lead to dangerous paths. Mobile phones, computers and smart innumerable inevitable components of present society like smart homes, smart cars and smart cards with their innumerable software applications in them would lead to unheralded, unheard and unthinkable psycho-social-moral anomalies in the society. For example using mobile phone while driving could have led to accidents, using social media in the internet have led to many divorces and the duplicating of the smart cards have been used by the hackers to withdraw personal bank accounts. This list of bad aspects of technology keeps multiplying. I never say that you should shun from technology. Today technology is a basic necessity. I do agree that the good part of present technology is more when compared to the bad part of the same technology. What I want is that, let there not be a state wherein any software app downloading would be a inclusion criteria as a mental disorder as per the Diagnostic Statistical Manual under American Psychiatric Association in their 6th edition. All bad parts of technology could be prevented if we have a means to handle these bad parts effectively by the innovated company start-ups and they provide the pure transparency and required adequate security from these agencies. This is how technology could infuse well to the society.

Before coming to the treble "X," sorry treble "EX," I have something interesting to talk. To tell you frankly, I do not know who coined the words? I had a friend whose argument was, "Why is a donkey donkey, not a dog?" I laughed at him. As our discussion was on a casual note, he did not felt bad. After few days, I was obsessed with his question. He was right in one way. What made my predecessor to call this particular animal a donkey?

I presumably think that he could have named this animal for two reasons. He could have been a monarch who named "Donkey" for which all his people in his kingdom should have agreed wilfully the name of this particular animal as Donkey. People going against the monarch's wishes would have been mercilessly killed. Hence, people out of fear just agreed to him and this word donkey is encrypted in our genes or he could have asked his counsels to mention as "Donkey" in the scriptures from then on. You and me are just following blindly and calling this particular animal that looks like a donkey as a donkey. If I call this animal by some other name, while others call this animal as donkey, today my head would not get chopped off, but people around me would take me to a mental hospital. This is one part of the story. Another part of the story is that probably this name with this particular animal should have some meaning. I explain what this donkey is about. This is 'a KEY to get things DONe'. This animal "Donkey" suits well to my explanation. Hence, today the words of any language have so many meanings hidden; your three-fold "Ex" too has such explanations.

Taking all these words into my consideration, first let me explain the word "Experiment." Inside the human minds laboratory of virtues, there is no word "Experiment" that exists. "Experiment" word exists within a scientist's mind but not within a peasants mind. This word is more affirmative. Hence, this word purchase time and would squeeze his intelligence. For a person of experience, this experiment does not work at all. This word "Experiment" works well with a neuro-psychologist than with a common man. This word suits well in a physical laboratory. Experiment always needs special gadgets, which when applied to humans by a neuro-psychologist should draw an inference, a specific inference from which we are sure of experimental applications. In chemistry and physics, these experiments are objective not subjective. Any product out from such experiments would possess a specific quality or properties, which can be measured. The virtues, which come out from our so-called psychological experiments, are impossible to measure. Hence, the word "experiment" is ruled out. As far as my knowledge extends, the virtue we learn out of experience is not from our experiments but actually they are the product of simple observations. This does not yield good fruits always but whenever our analysis and reasoning on observations in the medium of consciousness done well, then there is every possibility of yielding matured fruits to ripe well later. Once again, virtues are not good enough even after delivering the virtue fruits in our present system, but if it properly delivered in a basket of humanity, then our virtue seeds are properly ploughed in the society. Yes, here I would like to make a statement, "Uncertainty is not a certainty," fruits are certain. Hence, experience would always call for a simple observation, certainly not an experiment.

Another word, which I would like to highlight is the "Expectation." The expectation is a tricky word. To my knowledge, this word would try to explain the energy output of a person. This is to say that by Human Resource man, "How well I could extract psychological and physical power from employee." By this statement, you can gaze at the morality, which do not surface here. This word "Morality" lies with the people who expect the expectations of others. The experience does not comply with expectations. Any experienced man imbibes lots of virtues, who never expects anything from the society or his fellow people. Hence, trying to experiment on our experiences to get more expectations would lead to us to unnecessary stress. After all, "*Thaarsee* (roof)" in Kannada would mean stress in Psychology. An example is to imagine you are living in a house with a weak roof? Today, we have "Human Resources," a new department created by IT (information technology) and BT (bio technology) companies. I do not understand why they should be called "Human" when they expect expectations in terms of energy extraction from the individuals who get selected in these companies. According to me, humanity parallels with morality. These naive departments should be named as "Fit men and women selection department" rather than "Human resources department." A person who gets appointed by these companies in the Human Resources department is called as an HR. Therefore, HR's morality lies within his consciousness for the company's proprietor who had selected him. This is the exactly the reason why he looks to the energy levels (mental and physical) from whomever he selects for his mother company. Hence, my point is morality is the important pervading instrument to look in the expectations of all individuals. Unless, if this said instrument is not utilized and applied effectively in our society, then there could be a social anarchy. For example, frequent pink slips and throwing out of employees from the IT and BT sector by not stating any proper reasons. This is also true to our socio-economical culture of the society. Why should there be naxalism? Why should there be terrorism? Why should there be anathema?

You think deeply. In our earlier days, we had few notorious psychopaths. This psychopathic personality they had harboured probably because of their neuro-structural anomaly with consequent uninhibited morality. They were identified and punished as per the yesterday laws. The present scenario has changed. The criminality what you are talking now and the terrorism what we are really bothered about are the conditioned psyche, which could have been modified. Why did I say "Conditioned?" Only certain criminal conditions and psychopathic personalities come under psychiatric per se, many criminalities of criminals are basically secondary to environmental cues and by brainwash from few religious impotent. The quantum of criminality should come down with the increase in the quality of people's life and with their good education. This is exactly the opposite today. Hence, if my statement is true, then we are regressing in spite of the development. When this is the true nature of our present society, then where are we heading to? Can you find an answer for this? Hence, criminality and terrorism are the learned phenomena. Let us not blame the population growth, urbanization or development. It is the mind basically that is at fault, irrespective of socio-economic-psycho educational class. Our country does not possess colleges or universities preaching "Hate religion." We have universities to teach only religion. Religion is "Relay of humanity in a region." Hence, religion has been divided by us; religion did not had any division earlier. This is exactly the reason why I call it as "Learned phenomenon." Is this what you expected in your country? If you are highly meditative to your consciousness, then I would say it is the observation that imbibes virtues and values, not the experiment or expectations. I hope I have made my point clear to you.

MULTI DIMENTIONAL SENSES

"Doctor if you say that it is only the experience, experience alone, then does 'Experience' have any sixth sense or seventh sense?"

Really, a wonderful question, my friend. If you read Kannada, and if you have had a chance to read my first Kannada book, kindly read Manassu Mandara, and go through the topic "*Odedha Manassu,*" in which I have explained mind as, "Mind is a multi-dimensional projected image in time and space of a normal awake brain, which houses cognizance working on an ever-vibrating electrical activity. This electric activity is not static but always dynamic. The image produced is beyond the boundary, as the image is always expanding. The image evolved is relative or absolute and would always project on a continuous interaction with the existing matter." Hence, not sixth or seventh sense, as you have mentioned. We have only five senses. These five senses as per *Vedantha* restricted to body. Therefore, all together we have five perceptions. Adi Shankara asserted his view *Smrithi* as knowledge alone which is beyond our five senses. The perceiver would be mind, not the brain. As far as man is viewed, the senses I talk about ends here. The sixth or seventh sense is there for only execution of functions. The process of this executioner functions, according to me, is always multi-dimensional, rather calling with sixth or seventh dimensional senses. If we keep numbering the senses, people might even ask for eighth and ninth senses. This multi-dimensional executioner of sense is momentary and it is there for only good. This goodness could be to him or to the society, at large. For example, Thomas Alva Edison, who was deaf, had a multi-dimensional sense of inventing telephone. Wright Brothers through their multi-dimensional senses could invent the airplane. Socrates, with his multi-dimensional sense could say that his presence is only for good. Lord Buddha, from his enlightened multi-dimensional sense, could say, "We are all one." To this category, innumerable number of scientists, philosophers and enlightened teachers come under. The unfortunate thing is that the super senses taught by evil teachers preach miracles to happen. As long as people are fools, they keep listening to these sorts of stories. Miracle does happen with all of us only when there is an upward tilt from our thinking. Thinking de facto is creator's gift. Learning would refine thinking. Learning would not make thinking to super thinking. Super thinking is a product of enlightenment. This enlightenment is called as "*Prathiba*." This is light, and does not possess physical property but possess full of mysterious subtle senses. Hence, not exactly sixth and seventh senses that you are talking about. This particular *Prathiba* sense should possess multi-dimensional myriads of senses all over the space in time and inside the medium of consciousness. This multi-dimensional *Prathiba* is a waste, unless this *Prathiba* is used to execute a particular work by you. The divine light or the *Prathiba* do not arrive by just simple senses or by mere perception. This is like a *Masala Dosa* prepared out of a seasoned *Dosa* batter, good potato, nice onion and tasty *Chutney*. To explain it briefly, you perceive the senses and then these perceived sensory signals are carried to the central brain, where the signals are analyzed. After analysing, the signals are logically placed. Then they are discriminated and separated. The perceived idea thus formed after this separation would get mixed with memory and also with the learnt knowledge idea then changing to a thought. This thought could be a good or a bad thought. Leaving the bad thought aside, if you use this good thought to execute through your body machinery, you find a good *Masala Dosa* in your life. More you experience, more good the *Masala Dosa* tastes. All these steps would take place inside your brain with your knowledge. The mechanism is so fast you are not able to find out the previously mentioned process. Hence, experience and executors' functions are multi-senses, and we cannot gauze these instruments by with mere numbers like sixth or seventh sense. To make it simpler, when you find sixth and seventh sense people, they invariably practice or teach bad in the society. Those who practice only "Good" in the society have multi-dimensional senses to reach the needy. Frankly, these senses are well developed with animals. Humans do not possess these multi-dimensional senses but humans do possess good senses. Could you make out how many senses you have?

"I presume none."

"Me too."

OPEN MEDITATION

"Doctor, in what way meditation helps in building our own good senses?"

"What type of meditation, is it our usual meditation Yoga Teachers teach or I teach"

"Sorry I forgot, it is your Open Meditation"

In my second English book, "Paavithratha (the pure)," I have tried to explain the same as, "practice of neuro-psycho spiritualism." In my first official English book, "Parivarthna (the change)," I have explained the Spirit with its definition. Whenever I talk on Open Meditation, people get confused with my concept. Invariably, practice of meditation would mean closing the eyes and removing their bad thoughts. While doing so, they ask you to experience the bliss by stopping your thoughts, so as to merge your micro-cosmos with macro-cosmos. In this technique, while you are at relaxation, you are asked to remove unwanted thoughts from your brain. Subsequently, you are instructed to focus on a point of your interest. If somebody asks me to do the same, I would rather focus on a film actress than my wife. You want this? A wise man would state that "I am of the opinion that the quantum of offence for a criminal act holds same as to a criminal thinking." To explain the same in a different way "you should not be an abettor to your consciousness." As per my knowledge on Pathanjali's preaching's, his teachings were only on pure thinking. This is exactly what I would like to convey to you. Now, let me explain you what Meditation is all about. "Meditation is an attentive mind." When I divide this meditation word hypothetically, I would get Mind-Attention-Emotion. Attention is the principle factor here. Improving on our attention possibly would be able to find a solution to our negative emotions of our minds. In usual Meditation, an instructor when asks you to close your eyes, he probably would have an idea that you are more attentive. It is a myth. He has forgotten that the signals what comes within are most disturbing. Well he keeps on shouting at you like stop thinking "bad," stop thinking "bad." How is this possible? Because, according to me, there is nothing in this world to think only good. Thinking only "good" would not bring money and material. Without money, you cannot consult me. Hence, have bad thinking and then find a way to harness bad thoughts in your field of consciousness. You grow only bad plants. Remove dangerous plants and cultivate reasonable bad plants. You do tissue culture biotechnologically, so as to design good twigs and then add manure of knowledge to it. After doing so, go every day into your field of consciousness, and with your great attention try to search for fresh hybrid plants, which spurt out of this tissue culture. You practice to have a close observation with your eyes wide open. On a day-to-day basis you find a change (*Parivarthana*) in the plants. The bad plants are still bad plants. Here and there, you find a small twig possessing good fruits amid lots of bad fruits. To search these good fruits definitely, it would require you to haul your patience; this search would require your more energy and high attention with your eyes wide open. Now, be attentive what I am going to explain to you. In order to find a "good" with full of bad all over in the world requires good cognizance (skill) of yours. The one important function of many cognitive functions is Attention. This is exactly what Pathnajali Maha Rushi explains. In his *Sadhana Pada,* after asking you to practice the art of prior renunciation in his dossiers, he explains "*Chitthasya Bandha Dharanaa.*" Pathnajali Maha Rushi wrote this dossier with his eyes open. If he had closed his eyes, he could have not written this dossier. He would have had this thought while sleeping; therefore, to practice the art of meditation, one should practice meditation with their eyes open. Attention would increase with eyes open but not by closing eyes. Closing eyes probably would increase concentration momentarily. Can you close your eyes to increase your attention while driving a car? You know what happens next.

This is the only reason why I do not teach other meditations, I teach only Open Meditation. Lord Buddha never closed his eyes while he was meditating. So in my practice, if I close my eyes, how can I prescribe a medicine? By closing eyes, I might listen to the patient, but close observation of a patient's behavior is not possible. High attention and concentration would allow my mind for a right drug prescription. If a surgeon closes his eyes, what would happen to his surgery? Now I ask you to meditate what I say as Open Meditation in an affirmative path. This path is not simple. This path would require high energy levels. This energy is secondary to our mini-organic thermal power houses "Mitochondria." ATP-ase (arginine tyrosine phosphatase) synthesized from mitochondria is our true energy. The energy I am talking now is not found with certain people, they are the unfortunate people who have inherent problems with energy production units secondarily to gene malformation or acquired faulty powerhouse constructions. To whomever I am explaining this meditation technique, it is for those who are said to be normally manufacturing ATP-ase but faulty at utilizing this self-synthesized energy. I hope for all practical purposes, you have sufficient energy.

What is Yoga? Yoga originated from the word *Yajur*. Yoga is well documented and explained in "*Yajur Veda*." Practically speaking, what the world knows about the Yoga is a "simple mix." This is to say that mixing my nano-consciousness with the mega-consciousness of the Creators. I do not know the Creator. Hence, neither I am able to talk with Him nor I am able to mix my consciousness with His consciousness. Therefore, I know only Humans as God, not men. I firmly believe in Adi Shankara Charya's *Ukthi* (statement), the *Aham Brahmasmi* and *Thwam Asi*. What these two statements of His meant to us? The first statement is "I am supreme as my *Athman* houses my consciousness along with the consciousness of *Brahman*." The second statement would mean *Thwam* means *Brahman* and *Asi* is me. Hence "*Brahman* in me," so I am not "I." I am "I" along with "you." This is exactly what my Open Meditation stands for. In this type of meditative technique, I stand a chance in understanding you or in other words mixing with your mind and analysing your mind beforehand. An entrepreneur enjoys the fruit when he mixes customers consciousness early in order to make a particular deal to happen in a better way. This could be a possibility if entrepreneur opens his eyes with alertness. Otherwise, the deal would not be a possibility, if this entrepreneur had closed his eyes as a result of his daydreaming. The scale of money transaction is directly proportional to the attention of this entrepreneur, who had his eyes wide open or more aware. This is what I mean by the art of my Meditation or Open Meditation.

In psychiatry, it is not the prescribed drugs that cure the patient but how much we empathize with the patient. The empathy does miracles in life. Empathy is described in psychiatry textbooks as "getting into one's shoes." This is western teachings. East does not talk of "shoes" but talk only about mind (*Chitha*). This is to say how well we merge our myriads of senses with the other person's innumerable senses, or in another way, how well I mix my consciousness with the other person's and patients' consciousness. In this way, Pathnajali Maha Rushi taught us about the mixing. Mere thinking of the five senses of them or by me would not benefit a patient. I am not a "Precog" nor I am a "Nostar Damn." Our complicated life is not a fiction; life is a reality, truly speaking an object reality where our multiple of senses work. You know millions and trillions of signals impinge on our body daily. If this impingement on our senses is true, imagine how many sensory receptors have to work in our body. Can you count receptors in our body? It is like counting stars in the sky. Hence, always sixth or seventh sense is momentarily in a fight or flight situation. To fight or to flight, you have to keep your eyes open or keep your mind open. Eyes to which I am referring are for our body but the eye inside the mind is called as *Prathibha*. This *Prathibha* possesses not two eyes but several millions of eyes. To see the world, our two eyes are more than sufficient, but to observe, analyze and realize the mega *Brahman,* we have to have plenty of eyes. This is exactly what I call as "Multi-dimensional senses."

What does Open Meditation mean to our youth? Today, for any country to prosper, youth have to have enormous energy. They are like mitochondria of a cell. The crunch of economical problem to any country is their youth's unrest secondary to discontentment, despair and distress (three D's). The reasons, well they are like a woman's shopping list. For this, you have to read my earlier books Parivarthana (the change) and the Paavithratha (the purity). Keeping apart this subject, I would like to make a point here, which is worse than cancer and AIDS. It is the drug abuse. Drug abusers are not depressed but the energy levels that they have could have found a path of negativa. This is exactly what the sociologist Eric Sulleivan explains; this phenomenon is as dichotomy, honesty versus reality. Honesty is what we imbibe to people but the reality is that what they would have learnt in their life. Hence, keeping only honesty would presumably leave people in despair. This despair is the root cause for our faulty Meditation. This despair would have blocked their cognizance. This could have led to failure in their path of finding knowledge. This could be the only reason why Swamy Viveknandha in his Youth Movement programs asked youth to wake up or be "awake." What is this "awake?" This is not something in which you have to get up from night's sleep but what Swamy Viveknandha had meant was, "the youth to be more awake from their daydreams." Here I would like to restrict these daydreams to only obsessions. These obsessions in youth are fear of competition, fear for money to spend for their education, fear for getting a suitable job, fear for achieving their goals, fear for taking care of their families, etc. If you are rich, all these attributes does not work, but some other attributes could pinch their psyche. They are the desires, materials and enjoyments. Therefore, no youth in this present world is actually devoid of obsessions. This is where in our human march, my Open Meditation plays a key role, which when applied could help their mind for a *Parivarthana* (the change).

In *Vedantha*, the teachings of trio, *Drishta* (the subject), *Dreek* (the object) and *Dreeked* (the reason), stand testimony for our knowledge assertions. In *Pathanjali* Suthra, the teachings of trio, *Dhaarana* (the attention), *Dhyaana* (the concentration) and *Samadhi*(the contemplation), are the basic necessity for a person to achieve *Samyama* or the *Siddhi*(the fruit of power or knowledge). In my Open Meditation, I teach the same trilogy. Listen carefully, student is a subject, book is an object. His perception is on the matter (book), then what he infers out from such perception is the contemplation. Hence, for any student to be a good student, he should always attach to his object of study. Therefore, for a student to excel in this regard, he has to open his eyes. The effort, the patience and the energy are the three basic requisites for a good student. Here, I have purposely avoided ranking students. In our life, this rank does not bring everything but it is the art of life that does wonders to this confused society. To become a good student, one should have good observance, after observing he has to bring these observations to his consciousness. Inside his consciousness, he would reason it out before executing his functions. Can you do all these psychological attributes with your closed eyes?

Attention is a prerogative to perception. Book is there not to feel but to read. Reading requires opening of the eyes. You cannot close eyes? If you close your eyes, you are nowhere near the book. A mentally retarded also does see the book. They are the special people who are nice except to their parents. Nothing disturbs them except their hunger and special needs, which I and you cannot make out. They see the book but are unable to conceptualize because of their neuro-structural anomaly or for their poor development of brain. I would rather choose mentally retarded children than normal children who can bring all the problems like three "D's (drug abuse, deviance and defiant)" to their parents or problems they might pose to this society.

In brief, the many problems we are encountering today are "Three H's," inhumanity, lack of humility and absence of humbleness. Humanity is not an individual issue but it is a larger issue of religion, caste, sex and money. One percent of total populations are super rich who could own few islands. This indifference is more than sufficient to trigger a socio-economical atom bomb. Frankly, this bomb is just ticking to explode in a short time. The proportionate inequality could pose a huge unrest with the ninety-nine percent of population. This is worse than the terrorists exploding their explosives. In one percent of the population there exists humanity, which would be the only soul search for an effective future harmonious living. Presumably, a method where richness is divided and a portion of this division reaches to the poor would answer the essence of poorness. Please keep in mind, money will not answer all sorts of apathy and boredom of individuals.

Lord Buddha had said that possessing anxiety is as good as living dead. I am a psychiatrist, I see day in and day out the obsessive, rarely homosexuals and once a while constant anxiety patients; I know their pain and understand how much painful it is for them to possess. Lord Buddha also had said, "If you want to live, drop anxiety." My point is that just glancing through the Lord Buddha's book does not constitute Open Meditation. This technique will not reduce the anxiety by any means. Understanding the pain how you have gone through or understanding the pain others experiencing by you is Open Meditation.

Understanding our pain reduces our anxiety. Similarly, understanding somebody else's pain with sympathy reduces his pain. Students say, "I read a lot Doctor but fail in the exam." Yes, they are right. They read without making an effort to know what is written in the book. To constitute a process of Open Meditation is to make a little effort to know what is there in the book. Anyway, this explanation is not my purview but an educational psychologist would probably highlight the steps of knowing the art of reading. I have made a note in my first Kannada book, Manassu Mandara, where all first ten ranked players are on par with each one in any international tennis grand slam tournament but the patience and anxiety state of each player determines the winner for that day.

MIRACLE

"Doctor, you mean a student should not close his eyes?"

Why not! He should. Closing eyes would provide lots of concentration to the subject he had focused. Please know, it is momentary and closing eyes should not be for a long time. Closing eyes for a long time would allow other unnecessary thoughts to creep in. You close your eyes for more concentration and then open your eyes with more attention. This is exactly what my Open Meditation is all about.

"Doctor, you said Miracle, what exactly is this 'miracle'?"

I never talk on "miracle," because I do not know that this word "miracle" exits in my dictionary. To my knowledge, this word Miracle is a prime chapter with pseudo-people. These people are farce illusionists. Ignorant and innocent does fall pray for their illusionary techniques. Until now, whatever the miracles have been shown or explained are all science. You listen to the statements I make. This "miracle" never exists outside, it has to exist inside, this "inside" is my mind or in your mind. Show me a single miracle you know that is a "miracle." We are already living in this world that has arisen out of miracle. My existence is a miracle, my sound thinking is a miracle, my good feelings are miracles and my nice work is a miracle. My wonderful will when works under social structure is a miracle. The very nature, beautiful landscapes with green all around covered by mystique blue sky is a miracle. I am living surrounded by miracles; there is nothing to feel about the miracle. I am born, it is a miracle, I eat, it is a miracle, I live, it is a miracle, I marry, it is a miracle and I have children, it is also a miracle. Hence, miracle does not exist in the outside world; this miracle is present very much within my mind. In this world of divided families, a daughter chauffeuring *Uppittu* (south Indian breakfast delicacy) is a miracle. Wife meditating on her kitchen is a miracle. Husband who brings his earned money and parts with a part of his earning with his wife is a miracle. Wife not choosing to shop on that day is itself a miracle. An alcoholic finding his liver enzymes coming down after one month of his abstinence from alcohol is a great miracle. You name it, you have a miracle. There is nothing in this world that is not a miracle. In this world, beforehand, everything is present to say the miracle had happened. Next, what happens for good in this world is a miracle. This Nature does not enjoy the miracle, it is for you to enjoy the miracle for whatever happens well in the society. The visual treat of *Kailas Parvatha* is a miracle, the serenity of *Manasa Sarovara* in itself is a miracle. The wonderful world is a miracle. We are evil-minded people; we are born to disturb the ecological system of this world. Hence, by some means, if we are able to bring back the lost ecosystem of this world, it is a true miracle. Now, you tell where is this Miracle? This "miracle" is situated in me rather than in some shop for purchase. The very "change" in us and in this world towards goodness is a Miracle.

DIVORCE

"Doctor, could you explain divorce?"

This is a social evil. This is a social anomaly learnt on the "development" slogan. When you develop upwards by money and material, there also props up weird psycho-social problems. This divorce is one among many such developing social evils. Generally, development would mean construction of buildings for a common man. This is what universities do because we see only archaeological buildings but we never find internal builders who build our value system, virtues to deliver and knowledge to imbibe. This is exactly *Feku* disease prevailing in our country wherein universities feign as though these universities know all three said attributes. It is unfortunate to see that this word *Feku* has found a space in the Oxford Dictionary, where it means, for a department which feigns. What a parody!

Divorce is a word meant for "DrIVing out a person with fORCE." As a psychiatrist, this attitude I found with persons having immense bondage (strong relationships). This bondage could be a biological, social or legal bondage. It is easy to drive a son out or a father being driven out by his son. Though legality and society paves in, still the bondage between them is always strong. This is opposite with wife and husband. Therefore, a small force (small issues) automatically pops up with the couples to drive spouse out. One such force is "trust." Trust works only in relationships. We trust Gods, not wives. When I have trust in God, I have to have trust in Ghost too. Both are invisible. This is exactly why I say to "trust" those who is there in front of you, hence, trust "nature" who is in front of you, so also the wife.

In this social melee, temporary or permanent unrest develops with either of the two or both. When I say social, actually it is all the family members of either side, and they are upset from the divorce with anxiety and despondency. Hence, prospective study with suitable guidelines for this divorce is a necessity today. Courts are choked, lawyers are gagged and judges are burdened from these divorces. My point is how effectively we could be able to manage these divorces. Frankly, our effective managements have found a waste bin. The reasons for the divorces would probably be that the woman is educated, she is liberal, she finds a job or the opportunities for her are more now, she expresses her feelings freely and frankly, she feels men are patriarchs, she thinks men are machos, she is confused at the rate at which the world is changing, she is in a fix or stuck to comply social obligation or job conditions; likewise, many other psycho-social factors are playing as key roles to break the couple's relationship. Lastly, my Open Meditation does work wonders for those who have faulty non-verbal communication patterns, which is also an important factor from many factors when divorce is the answer. This sort of communication could be observed and eradicate while our eyes are wide open in any given relationship. Many a time people make derogatory non-verbal signs; which are painful, such faulty signs one could notice when eyes are open, not when eyes are closed, and therefore immediately a solution is drawn to minimize the foreseen misunderstandings. This is exactly how my Open Meditation works.

My Open Meditation does have any role at all here? When each divorce increases or boosts into innumerable psycho-social factors, my Open Meditation could be a choice to manage. I explain why I said so. Today, each child in our family is precious. The reasons obviously are the financial crunch of rearing many children and couples reduced effort of providing their offspring's maximum comforts, physically as well as psychologically. As reasons are glaring more and more, nuclear families pop up. Keeping this view today, man avoids difficulties in life. He expects life should sail smooth. Today, palatable water in this world is less in quantity when compared to non-palatable water. Hence, what we find minimum in this world is most turbulent. The present large population stirs the available little palatable water dirtily through their unrest minds. Their primary objective is to stack the palatable water more and more. Therefore, each child is provided with lots of care, lots of material and lots of wealth, so to say, pampered. Children are being constantly watched and snub the free flow nature in them. The child's playing wings are cut for limited activity. The present-day child has the lacuna of playing with other children belonging to the same family, as families are getting divided and divided. The natural green inside of their compounds has been converted into restricted lawns. The child has to play within the space provided. Parents do not allow their children to play with other children for the fear of getting contaminated not by germs but with probably the ills of other child who could be harbouring them. It is just the obsessions we possess or fear we have. We are not animals to give birth and then to forget after a brief post natal period. For the present socio-economic conditions, politico-legal nature of the various countries, cultural and traditional values of any country, bondage, and relationships of each country, etc. are affecting rearing or bringing up a child, and this is becoming more difficult. In this regard, each modern child is losing psychological immunity against mild stress that a child could come across when he or she grows up.

CONFUSED YOUTH

Doctor, how could you help youth through your Open Meditation?

These children after growing up in this narrow-minded world, the youth is a confused angry man. Naturally, the growing gap between young enthusiasms to elder's restrictions are taken care by parents when the youths were put in to this world of chaos. There is no other option for the young to escape from the hard reality, which he or she is going to face. We have no under-graduation colleges that teach *Samsara* (life). The youth is very good at mathematics or English but fails in the life. In this situation, when young finds the hard reality of life, his or her mind does not get hardened. Brain is soft not hard when compared to other parts of the body. If by chance, the brain loses its sheen of softness, the young could present with different neurological disorders like epilepsy. In psychiatry, at molecular level, the stress we encounter would lead to neuro-chemical changes, and hence anxiety with three D's, they are despair, despondency and depression. Young mind is nascent and is always like gas. Gas disperses and disappears but not the cotton frill, which only floats in the air, never disappears. This is exactly what I would like to convey to youth that the young should not be like a gas but should find a place like a cotton frill to float and royally come down to earth finally. World is beautiful and wonderful. Yes, the young are not birds but have to place their feet firmly on the ground, and young never dwell above the earth. The young should have some means to make the mind light, so that he can fly by mind not by body; the latter would lead to injuries, as he has no wings. The meditative methods, which a youth could meditate, I have narrated in my second English book, Paavithratha (the purity). To be brief, this book mentions types of meditation, how Nachiketha could be free from the ignorance, which he had possessed after he came in contact with Lord Yama, who had explained him the true nature of *Brahman*. How Lord Buddha could fly like a Humming bird after he got freed from worldly attachments. How he could make people listen to the compassionate music by playing the percussion instruments of "forget" and "forgiveness." I do not say that the young should become *Sanyasi* (monk) or *Sanyasini*. If they are, as a psychiatrist, I should rethink about their mental status. Hence, what I wanted them to be is to adopt a way where they could reduce their stress by using available worldly psycho-social resources near to them. To give some examples—due to generational gap, a young never listens to his or her parent's advice. If this is the issue, a student who actually has a learning disorder insists on professional course. A student joins these courses on his or her insistence. For parents, the real problems start after these students join the courses of their choice. Here role of mental health professionals comes into play. In this situation, I try my Open Meditation to the student and his or her parents. The technique, which I narrate, is very simple. This is a fusion technique like music fusion. I always try to fuse students mind with parents mind and vice versa. This is the only way for the student's mind to know his or her parents' minds and the opposite is also true. Student would have joined the professional course by paying a hefty donation. I ask students to mix his mind with his parents and see what they have inside their mind affirmatively and I ask the same for the parents to view their son or daughters' mind with compassion. I ask them to practice over a period of days. The time they spend every day would be five minutes. Initially, their task is to observe them with a mind full of attention. After this attentive mind, their other task is to mix the individual's consciousness to make an effort to know the respective minds before the start of their complete observations. Invariably, every parent would have observed whether their children had locked their rooms from inside or not, observed incoming and outgoing calls in their children's mobile phones, they would have observed the accessibility to their internet websites, they would have observed their children playing different types of games in their mobile phones, they could have observed their children's behavior and anatomy of their friendships, they would have made a note of recent behavioral changes, they could have made an observation in their children's mood, they could have observed which serial in the TV they watch, they could have found any substance abuse he or she indulged in, etc. My teaching is that before parents act on their children's negative acts and negative thoughts, they should have been assessed beforehand by my Open Meditation Technique. For example, a student should go and chat with his father before his father says "no" to him for joining to a professional course. The misunderstanding or the arguments between father and student son could probably be due to this "no." If these students have a mechanism to mix their minds with their father's mind for a presumable reason to say this "no," there could not have been many arguments or quarrels with antecedent misunderstandings. The reason behind for these "no's" could be two reasons: that his son is not up to take the challenge of a professional course or the other reason could be money crunch. The same example holds good for the parents. An example would be that for parents to try and explain or address their student child's mind for not being able to sustain finances for such courses. The reason with the student could be probably learning disability observed by the parents. Parents should have congruent advisory plan or rewards plan towards their wards. I too agree that all are not professionals, but as a psychiatrist, I teach this art of Open Meditation to the student and his parents. By my Open Meditation, parents and children would have to come to know each other's mind beforehand to decide whether to join or not for technical or professional courses.

Why I should call this as counselling, I would rather call what Pathanjali taught us as Yoga, which is very much *Desi* (native). This art is ours; hence, I call this technique as Yoga after my own understanding on Pathanjali yoga *Suthras*; in English, I calls this as Open Meditation. When I was doing psychiatry, these *Desi* teachings were not taught to me by my teachers. Of late, I believe they have a department of Yoga, which is restricted to pseudo-Yoga. I feel strongly that they better remove this Yoga from their board and re-write as *Yoga Asana*. Their way of meditation is done on closed eyes, I oppose. Closing eyes does not work. Open eyes does work. Closing eyes would allow a patient to relax. A relaxing mind does not give food, and prevent quarrels, misunderstandings and boredoms. Relaxing comforts a man. Relaxing with open eyes and meditating on the event would prevent many problems we face today. Problems could be from any quarter of life. This could be adjustments, finding a job to earn and searching for resources near to our reach. Interactions could be between the various relationships, between customer and provider as in entrepreneurship, between man and nature for effective ecosystem and between man and animals in this losing battle. The intention of My Open Meditation is very ideal in a one-to-one relationship (for example-couple), where a process of conscious mixing takes place beforehand, in which neither dominance nor submission materialize, materialization through understanding has to take place to bring harmony for a stress-free future life. Therefore, my technique would largely help the members of a family, people in the office or in the society. My Open Meditation would also help those who are in close relationships for their lasting maintenance. My technique would be a gateway to enter directly into one's mind and visualize the mind inside with one's *Divya Jyothi* (the mind eye).

SPIRIT

"Doctor, spirit, does it exist?"

Definitely, "spirit" exists only for fools. It does not exist to a man of wisdom. I have come across in my practice vivid narrations on these spirits. I would like to clear the concocted vibration of many worshiping places. These vibrations we talk today are equal to spirits. Frankly, people want a change, hence, they seek worship places to come out from their mundane. A psychiatrist consultation would be costly to many patients. Hence, they go in search of worshiping places. It is their money and their choice. They never go to any temples, which are located deep in the deep woods. This is exactly what I would like to convey. The clean sanitation or the good infrastructure in the form of potable water and nice food to eat are the basic necessities for anybody to dwell. For somebody to dwell within their mind, they have to have pure thinking and good reasoning. When thought that as one of the basic four functions of the mind and reasoning is one among many cognizance of mind are not functioning properly your "spirit" automatically haunts within. These people who are haunted with the said "spirit," who have an intention of getting rid of their spirits, would approach places of Vibration. I was told by many, "Sir, have you visited Mylara Lingeshwara temple. The God is a *Uddbhava Murthy* (grown from the ground) sir. Please visit sir, you get enormous power." I told him, "Yes, I have visited this temple many times. You would like to have a fight with me. I have powers given by this God, should I hit you." He laughed and disappeared from my scene. You should not assume that I do not believe in the "spirit." I am a moderate rationalist; I am here to explain only the good part of the "spirit," not the bad part of the spirit. Today, what we talk on Vibrations are because of the good spirit within us. For this, why should one seek Vibration from somewhere when it is already present in you. You are going to many worshiping places because it is a cultural compulsion forced on you. If we deviate from this socially accepted compulsive norm in a society, we are called as "atheists," and if we follow then as "believers." I go to a temple because my wife asks me to go. If my late father had asked me to do the same, I would not have done this because I was young. Hence, I am an "atheist"". In this confusion today, I am clear in my mind. I follow what society says because I respect my cultural values and traditional virtues. Whatever I narrate is purely my thinking and more on a psycho-social science perspective. I hope you had read my first English book Parivarthana (the change). I have explained what Spirituality is? To be brief or to refresh, "It is a science that deals with the high nature of the mind without consuming the spirit (alcohol)." Hitherto, it is seen that man is high only after substance abuse. My point is, why a man should not be high without alcohol. The study of this "high nature of mind without substance abuse" is called as Spiritualism.

The spirit what we speak today does come to the mentally ignorant people. This sickness is not true sickness of mind. Mentally sick would visit or would have visited mental health professionals. The sickness of mind I am talking is for the people who are "common people," who are not worthy to be born in this world of socio-economical inequality. As a tax-paying common man born to this country, his freedom been hijacked, his voice has been silenced and his human values are shattered. In this world, thirty-five percent of people are unfortunate to get even basic human rights what a human being is entitled to. Whose mistake is this, should I call this as a social anomaly or the problem with my country's spirit?

Without our instinctual urge, imagine where we would have been or simply we would not be living in this world. My explanations are all confusing. It is a parody. It is not the nihilism for our survival. This nihilism is a good word for the people in the towns and cities but not for the people who live as tribals deep inside the Amazon forests. This is exactly the reason why tribals do not suffer from mental depressions. They have mental illnesses in the form of "spirits" acting on them due to their pure ignorance. Ignorance withers away with knowledge. This knowledge increases our boredom, despondency and dysphoria but not the true mental illnesses. Mental illnesses are secondary to neuro-chemical changes of neuronal cells. When a man in his endeavour tries to seek minimal needs of his life, he naturally submits himself for the created spirits by the opportunistic people around him, because he is depressed and dejected. Hence, he wants an immediate happiness; this is how he falls prey to innumerable bad "spirit" mongers and ultimately he would double his sufferings. People laugh at me if I make any statements on these disgusted spirits. Many blessed by spirits join politics only to stack their ill richness with these half-baked self-styled Gods. Their powers (politicians and self-styled Gods) rise on an algebraic sum. As I live with simple arithmetics, I ignore the "spirit" what ignorant people talk. The good spirit stands only for our value systems, and then are delivered as virtues for the suppressed, repressed and depressed people of society. Except few, I hardly hear or see the spirit from the rich and famous.

I was asked once by a fellow traveller in a bus, "Doctor do you believe in spirits." This question he could ask me after he had developed liking my Open Meditation narrations. He is a technical man who was about to board a flight to go abroad for pursuing a master's degree. There is an interesting story behind his question, because he had mastered his degree in sound system or music system. One day, he wanted his family members to hear the invisible spirit probably living in his house. This spirit concept came to him after watching movies of haunting spirits. He wanted to test whether his house too was haunted from such spirits. For this, he manually assembled ultra-modern mike and speakers in his backyard. He switched his ultra-designed mike system on in his hall at midnight twelve and then went and took a good sleep. Next morning, he wanted to test the spirit, which has dwelled in his house. To his surprise, he could hear the anklet sound. He was sure of the spirit living and made his family members to believe the same. From that day, all family members went sleepless. Few of his family members consulted family physicians who drubbed them nonsense and this techie consulted a neurologist too, who had prescribed sedatives to him; consuming these pills left him with side effects. Hence, he had stopped consuming prescribed drugs. Their interest on Ghosts never stopped. In search of these spirits, his friends, colleagues and family members woke up till midnight to find. They had maintained utmost silence to find the spirit. They searched inside and outside of this techie's house to find the said spirit. They could not catch. He even thought of consulting a *Desi* ghost buster (*Manthra Vaadi*). After wise interference from his elders, he had stopped approaching the *Manthra Vaadi*. Therefore, he tried to influence his spirit on me. I had listened to his story and asked, "Did you try your machine simultaneously outside and inside your house at midnight." The answer was "no." I had explained him, "You try this and come back to me." I did give my music album as a token to him for this patient listening to my Open Meditation. I am sure he would not contact me. Because the spirit what he was talking is not at all a spirit. Listen why?

As per science, the space is not empty or vacuum. The space is filled with pockets of energy. The energy is very little to burn a zero candle bulb for a fraction of second. The movement of this energy is not constant and is always moving. Some parts of space are full of energy and some other parts of space are not filled even with little energy. The invisible matter does contain electromagnetic waves, which light up a low watt electric bulb. Hence, these electromagnetic waves make noise possessing very minimal decibels, which could not be heard by normal ear. This techie had designed such a powerful mike and speakers that any noise created (anklet noise) after the movement of energy was picked and played. The same phenomenon is called by few as "spirits," some call it as "vibration" and I call this as "science." Hence, spirits is for the ignorant, vibration is for the pseudo-spiritualist and science is for the man of known. Therefore, the negative spirit should change to an affirmative science with positive mindful vibrations. The possibility of knowing would be from open mindedness of a man and "positive" and "negative," what the ignorant speak about, are from their probable narrow mindedness. This is exactly what my Open Meditation is all about.

WORLD OF FOOLS

"Doctor, I saw you the other day in the temple performing *Homa* and *Hawana* with your wife. Would this ritual made any difference in you?"

Man born in this midst of fools is a big fool. I do not mean that no birth should take place on this earth. When a fool is born, earth suffers because this fool born spoils our earth's ecosystem. Mother Earth is compassionate and she never differentiates wise and the fool when she gave birth to her children. We are all born good, as we grow up we become fools because fools live around fool. In this world of fools, I am a big fool, because for all the good knowledge I possess, I am not able to impart any knowledge to the people around me. It does not mean that I am an enlightened master. In the yester years, the enlightened masters were killed when they had used knowledge as their tool of spreading only good. Today a modern rationalist thinker has met the same tragedy. Because of this reason, a knowledgeable person never calls himself as a person of known but he would like to be called as moderate by his fellow people. A fool is not different from a religious ritualistic man. I am not ritualistic, generally people are ritualistic, but I believe in religion than in rituals. Today *Homa* and *Hawana* are there only to bring cheer but not the powers. This *Homa* and *Hawana* do not bring any miracle but miracle could happen when we meditate on this *Homa* and *Hawana*. As per *Vedhantha*, performing *Homa* is an obeisance and an obligation for a man born to Hindu Religion. Yes, I am lucky to be born and not so lucky because I am placed in the midst of invented innumerable religions. I would be doubly lucky if am placed in the midst of the universal religion. After all, "religion" originated from a Latin word "religere," which is meant to share. Hence, sharing tradition and culture in a defined region is called as "religion." As I am in a region called as Indus; as days passed by I became an Indi. As this word got hammered by many generational Hindi-speaking people, this Indi was designed into Hind. So, any person living in this Indus Valley became naturally Hindu. Generally, speaking irrespective of any religion, man living in this Indus Valley is called as an Hindu. It does not matter whatever different religions practice their faith, but they are always Hindus. Coming to *Homa's* parse, we light a sacred pyre and as obeisance man offer ghee, different medicinal plant twigs, pulses and other items to please Lord Agni Deva (God fire). Pundits would say, by doing so you are offering your wealth to invisible Gods. They also say that *Homa* is like a post office wherein money transfers from one post office to a distant post office. How mean are we because if we offer money to the fire everybody presumes what would happen to the money we have offered. It just melts away. Therefore, people part cents and not dollars. People are very intelligent by doing so, because money they spend is to burn their stomachs with intake of alcohol for their highs. As long as this money does not belong to me, why should I bother for the money that belongs to someone? If this ritualistic *Homa* and *Hawana* were parcels for our offerings to Lord from Earth to Heaven, many patriarchs would have parcelled their spouses long back. This was in vogue as an easy way of silencing the women in our religion. This is exactly the reason our statutory Law was strengthened against the immoral natural Law that existed in our medieval time. Hence, my point is, we should not burn the sacred pyre or our stomachs, but we should always fire the mind to burn the things that possess sinister means. I think you have read my first Kannada book Manassu Mandara under the topic *Homa Havanagalandare*, where I have written a poem on *Homa*. Lord Krishna, in the epic Mahabharata, has explained the reason behind these *Homas*. He had asked Arjuna to burn the Ego and Fear for a right cause to uplift the *Dharma* (properties of society). Hence, we should celebrate *Homa* and *Havana* to burn our egos, so as to refresh our human values and virtues often. All these rituals have symbolic picture but the wise always keeps burning his popping evils on a day-to-day basis inside his mind towards gateway of *Moksha* (little liberation). This is a good way of performing *Homa* and *Havana* inside our mind rather than performing outside, thus preventing pollution, saving money and dispelling ignorance. I am sure the rooster who makes noise ignorantly will not like my explanations. Yes, you are right. I was there along with my wife. I cannot part away from my wife you see!

PRACTICE OF OPEN MEDITATION

"Doctor, our usual practice of Meditation is that to meditate on closed eyes, you ask us to open our eyes and meditate, I am confused Doctor?"

Yes, we live in confusion. The first confusion a man can have is confusion between morals we learn from our parents and from our teachers as young and immoral practices we adopt to live when we attain adulthood. Mind is always riddled with confusions. There are no known self-apparatuses within us to correct this confusion. Hence, we keep seeking different apparatuses or instruments to sort out our confusions. To name few of these apparatuses, we could seek for counselling from health professional, ask advice from near ones or we might meditate with the knowledge as to what meditation would mean. Counselling and advice come in handy, they are not expensive, and especially eager friends and relatives do this and they claim they did a great job. After this work done, from inside they curb him "yes, he deserves this." Meditation is one thing, which does not come handy. Many meditating centres are like kitty parties. They are small clubs. People should be members to this club. To take a membership in these clubs, it is at the hands of the existing members. They can refuse or include the new member. Real professional clubs allow anybody who pays money or has some status and the power he possess. I do not have all these three, hence, I could not join any of these *Swamy* (modern Guru's) clubs. In my first

English book Parivarthana (the change), I have explained in length the meditation I follow. I am vehemently opposed to practice this closed eyes' meditation. There are two reasons, which I would like to explain. One thing is that this meditation technique is done indoors (enclosed chambers) and the next thing is to practice the same outdoor, we have to have time and place. Indoors, we are partially choked with the exhaled CO_2 (Carbon Dioxide) by the people who are gathered there. They do not ask you to meditate but they ask you to inhale and exhale air. You inhale less O_2 (Oxygen) and exhale more CO_2. Therefore, for all practicality you are taking CO_2 instead of pure oxygen. I do not ask you to take literally my narrations. I am just explaining the science behind these things. People feel that I am satirical. Listen to this why? You show me one poor or a farmer who had joined these time-consuming kitty parties doing Yoga. A poor would not be admitted to these kitty parties because he is poor and a farmer could not become a member as he is always doing the Open Meditation in his field. If a farmer closes his eyes and meditates, we all start starving. Therefore, just Meditation is only for the rich and famous. As I explained earlier, the carbon dioxide we inhale invariably makes mind to get confused. Hence, the meditation that the kitty party members practice is not true meditation. The meditation what they should practice should be in their interactive spaces not in the enclosed space. In this interactive space, there is nothing like closing eyes. If a kitty party member closes his eyes while interacting with the outside world, this member would succumb to injuries. It is like driving a car with closed eyes. Hence, the foremost quality for a meditative member should be that he should possess high quality of watchfulness. Breathing does not produce awareness but oxygen in his breathing is a precursor for his increased attention. Speedy breathing is a hinderer for good attention because this technique acidifies the blood. The mere confusion in a person would acidify his blood from hurried breathing. Hence, one should breathe slowly while reacting to the reality. When you meditate inside an enclosed chamber, this practice would not help your cognizance. For a good cognizance, one should have Patience, Persuasion and Perseverance, which are available outside the chamber. I may be wrong to say that all these three "P's" are not the properties of kitty party members. These three P's are the properties of the outside world. I am also apologetic to these kitty party members for their possession of three attributes. They are presumably Poverty of thoughts, Poor knowledge and Probable happiness. Once again, these are also three "P's." Compare these three P's to the earlier three P's, you can find a difference between three P'S of ordinary meditation to the three P's of my Open Meditation.

Closed eye meditation is very much a subjugated matter. Because the benefits of this type of meditation is highly debatable as their explanations are more subjective in nature and are more philosophical individually. My Open Meditation is more science oriented and objective in nature. I have come across ICMR (Indian council for Medical Research) sponsoring the few acclaimed to have powers of meditative practices to come out with some papers on their closed eye meditation. What a waste of money. The same money could have been used as subsidies to the farmers.

The basic principle behind preaching meditation with closed eyes is that the man would have shut all incoming signals through his five senses and he lights up his inside light to know what he is. This technique is otherwise called as *Adhyathma* or the art of knowing self. The funny part of this practice is that one can close his eyes, and can he close his skin, ear, tongue and nose? Imagine if you try to close your nose and mouth. You shout "Hell to meditation." This is impossible for anybody to practice meditation by closing our nostrils and mouth but this *Adhyathma* (inward journey) could be a possibility for a person who practices *Prthyahara* of Pathnjali. They are the true seekers, as I am not, I cannot practice this art of meditation. I am just a seeker; hence, I am able to practice only Open Meditation. As a seeker, I seek only what is important to me. When I divide this "importance," I divide it into two. One is important life attributes to live and another is important observations, which are necessary for my knowledge and for my skill to dwell in the society. To make it simpler, first is the "life quotient" for my relationships and next is the "intelligent quotient" to earn for my living. When your wife is packing her belongings from your house, can you meditate by closing your eyes? You have to hug your wife and kiss her from your heart. This requires eyes to be open. This is a momentary period; if you miss you are gone. This is what I mean by "life quotient." When your house is burning, you cannot close your eyes and meditate expecting some miracle to happen. Our life is not a movie. We are living in a reality bioscope, not in a fiction multi-scope. Hence, it is your skills that play a key role to arrange immediately the available resources to douse a fire. This is exactly why I call as "our presence of mind "or our "intelligent quotient," which helps us at the neck of the moment. This never happens in many because invariably we go for a shock, and in this state, there would be depersonalisation and derealisation (post-traumatic stress disorder), hence, we are not able to act. To avoid this state we should learn the art of Open Meditation.

A woman who was at the verge of getting sexually abused or harassed should have had used her inner learnt mechanisms to know the harassing persons mind beforehand to avoid or to escape from him. The girl need not empathize with attacking people and submit her body to them joyfully to meet their needs, as some Semi-Gods professed; basically, avoiding them is an art using her many innate learnt skills. Empathy stands fit for professionalism. This Open Meditation is a technique, which everybody can learn if they wanted to avoid stressful situations. My method of meditation can be adapted in any hostile atmosphere. Hence, in this technique, I ask you to have a high level of attention with minimum anxiety, moderate trust and maximum self-belief.

FIRE

"Doctor, as per Buddha, desire or *Sukha* is the reason behind sorrow or *Dukha*, what would you say?"

You have asked an interesting question. Fire is innocent. We all evolved out of fire. Without sun, we all will perish. Sun is a symbol of fire. We are not living in Antarctica. People in Antarctica eat uncooked meat but they do require fire for their tea. Hence, fire is universal and represents saffron colour, which explains the all-inclusive ability of fire, because fire in saffron and knows only to hug all to impart reasonable comfort. There is no logic how we transport our material to God or to our Ancestors after obeisance through *Yagna*. This is exactly why our politicians and bureaucrats burn the important secret documents in their office when they are caught by CBI on corruption charges. This is a burning problem to a taxpayer in our country. They are so thick and firewalled that they never learn the true nature of fire from our *Vedantha*. With all my innocence to explain "desire," I have only narration than definition. The "desire" is like "self-fire." The "life smoke" is satisfactory, as in this temperature smoke allows a person to live, but real fire does not allow man to live. This is exactly why I would like to convey that the desirous people burn themselves. It is not second or third degree burns, burning with "in"; this burn affects the mind and heart. Mind does not get weird or heart does not get blocked but the anxiety behind the desire would lead to immature death like in slow poisoning except in few individuals who are named after "Psychopaths." Here morality or the guilt never finds any space in their brains. This could be the reason why they are called as "moral maroons." Ironically, as we all are moving in this world at a fast pace or the information technology is galloping at a lightning speed of late, we have found people with similar analogy with different names as "Selfy Maroons" and "Video Maroons." Today, the word "selfie" has found a place in Oxford Dictionary but failed to find the place in a legal dictionary. Man is dying, we want a selfie in front of a dying person, person has lost his limb and we click the video instead of taking traumatized person to a nearby hospital. The desire to live and desire to let and live are the basic necessities of a man, in the similar fashion desire to offer help is more human. Hence, for a man to live, *Sukha* (happiness) should have learnt the art of no self-desire, if he is desire full only *Dukha* (sorrow) remains throughout. This is exactly what Lord Buddha taught us!

DEVOTION AND DESIRE

Doctor, what could be the meaning of devotee? Can you explain?

A person devotes himself to a particular God is layman's explanation of devotion. Listen to my explanation. Now I split this word "devote." After splitting, I got two split words "De + voting." For a particular party to come to power, we have to vote a party to majority. This is satisfactory for a party but not for God; God never asks for an election or asks the people to vote him. Hence, as we never vote any particular God, we have selected and elected the God without any contest. Hence, we all have elected a single God but the parody is that we are quarrelling for in numerable Gods. Devotion should be to one God and this God is my Goodness. Hence, my sincere advice to you is that you should devote to yourself.

This is my personal explanation; do not try to search meaning for this word "devote" in any books. The same analogy does hold good also for "desire," that is "De + ire." The meaning to "ire" is provoking. For our humanitarian desire, we have to have disrespect to this "ire." This disrespect (De) to "ire" is "desire." Therefore, this word looks to me as paradox wherein this word is used in a different context altogether. To put this in simple terms, "stop desire." This is what our poorly equipped *Swamys* preach. How we can stop our desire, if I stop my desire I should not live here, I should live in the forest eating grass and wild fruits. I am vegetarian you know, having stopped being a non-vegetarian long back. The desire should be a desire to pursue the life but not the desire to conquer. This sentence has enormous meaning. Desire to live is an accepted norm but desire to conquer is not acceptable, except in the battlefield. This "conquer" has different conations. For me, they are possession of ill wealth, possessing pseudo-pride and sticking to power. These items keep growing like a woman's shopping list. For a wise man, this "conquer" word has different meanings. Wise is wise because he has conquered virtues, values and vision. See, the three "V's" that have tremendous impact in our life. Possessing these three "V's" would enhance your realization. This realization would bring a change in this world of bioscopy. The same realization does not find any place in the illusionary world. The desire what every one of us could think would find a slot only in the illusionary world. As soon as this word "desire" finds a place in the illusionary world or with the great *Maya,* the *Dumbana* (fear) automatically crops up. The only way to escape this "ire" or the wrath is to find a change in us from "desire" to "wise." Hence Lord Buddha was one person who could come out from the royal atmosphere to *Shoonya* environment. This could be the reason why Lord Buddha never experienced *Dukha.* You want this state; you can, when you drop all belongings in front of me now, do not disrobe, do the same from your mind.

Doctor, more on "desires" please.

In *Vedantha,* the desire is more of a *Viparyaya* or the mental image. In western books, the same is called as the mindset. In this mindset, "desire" has a place within a relative reality. Desire could find a place in absolute when this desire stands straight to virtues. A man is remembered not for his money but for his virtues. Man leaves wealth for somebody to enjoy but he leave virtues for others to emulate from his deeds. Pathanjali has said that the seeds of Desire would burn away when non-organic manure like greed, wealth and dishonesty are used, seeds could be grown to its full potential when organic manure like values or virtues are used while sowing in the field of one's soul.

Desires and aspirations are almost equal but both have the potency to increase anxiety. I am desirous and have many aspirations, but in this world of competition, I might not achieve the goals what I have to. Possessing goals are prerequisites of aspiring students, but to meet these goals, students have to struggle in this competitive world. In spite of the Supreme Court order to free highways with humps, still we are unable to make highways free of humps. Therefore, whatever the effort Government policies are making for smooth running of the education system in our country, we are facing innumerable bumps from the wealthy educational institutions coercing with peoples representatives. The socio-economic crunch students could face and psychological pressures the students undergo also bear bad in our educational system. If you have money, it does not mean that you get a better or best educational system, which is a myth. I agree that a meritorious student feels the pinch of reservations, exorbitant institutional charges and the money a student has to spend in our educational system. We are going wayward from the *Vedanthic* teachings. These teachings were from real *Guru* and *Chela* teachings. It was an obligation of the *Guru* to impart knowledge to their pupils. Today, there are no obligations but *Guru* would oblige his teachings to his pupil against money. We are changing, but in this dichotomy, the real *Guru* is one who has full of his desires, ambitions and aspirations for his student to attain the highest moral standards and the knowledge. Moral standards a student learns is Life Quotient and the knowledge a student acquires is Intelligent Quotient. When there is split in these two quotients, the desires, ambitions and aspirations of this particular student would burn away with excessive desires. This is all I know about your "desire."

"Doctor, does your Open Meditation have any role in burning 'desire'?"

My Open Meditation has tremendous role for not burning the desire but it has a role to become desireless. As I have already explained to you that "desire" is "self-fire," then how could you burn a fire, which already exists. No one lit a fire. Hence, there is a possibility of free-fire state. This you could achieve when eyes are open but not by eye closing. If your car catches fire, you cannot close your eyes. If you close your eyes when your car catches fire, you do not escape. Similarly, you do not like "self-fire." To come out from this fire, you have to meditate on your fire. The meditation techniques you require to escape from your own fire are by finding the modes and means of living and progress. A singer can close his eyes while he sings but not an accompanying artist who plays an instrument. Here also, the same version does apply. If we close our eyes (not literally), how will we find the available resources in front of us to douse our excessive fire. With your fire, you have achieved everything but from the excessive fire you have, you could burn your fingers. Hence, to neutralize the same, you should run around to find a good doctor, a psychiatrist. After burning your finger, if you close your eyes, you mean you do not experience the pain it produces! No, sleep is not the protector of fire. All of us have burnt our fingers knowingly or unknowingly before we reach certain stage or position in our life. Hence, we burn our fingers seemingly by accident. In case of "desire," we burn our mind wilfully and get caught in the Maya's net. You are finished; you are like a fish caught in a net. Fish cannot escape the net because it is devoid of hands and legs, it does possess, but they are useless because they are meant only to swim but God is so compassionate to you by providing hands with skill and legs to run. Hence, no man on earth can run with closed eyes except a magician or a trickster. Hence, the word "desire" stands to disembark from fire. This can be done only by "Attentive mind for our emotions" or the Open Meditation.

IRRITABILITY AND OPEN MEDITATION

"Doctor, when I was sitting in your chamber sipping tea, there was a student who wanted counselling for his irritability from you, strange I was irritable in my young days, never consulted any professional. What is 'irritability' then?"

A good question you asked me. Kindly do not take my explanation at its literal plane because my narrations might look something funny to you. If I explain this "Irritability" in my sphere, I ask you to concentrate for what I say. The "irritability" is a state where we smear table salt to an already existing irritating patch of itch. This problem of itching asks you to consult dermatologist. You go to any medical college anywhere in this country, you see departments of dermatology and department of psychiatry having common corridors. These departments are present side-by-side or facing each other face-to-face in the same corridor. I was wondering why these two departments have such an affinity between them. I was able to understand these two departments proximity when I was able to make a comparison for the obsession of scratching to an itch and the compulsion of the mind to which the man scratches his whole body (in certain psychiatric conditions like external zoopathy. In this condition, man is deluded with worms all over his body. This is one form of kinesthetic hallucination). Here the common factor is "scratch" but the causes are different, one is in body and another is in mind. My body is nerved all over with a complex matrix of neuro-receptors, neuronal cells, neuronal tracts, neuronal plexus, neuronal centres and myriads of neuronal functional areas inside our brain and with their thousands of highly interactive neuro-hormonal transmitters. Therefore, in this matrix, the itch at the periphery allows a person to scratch his mind, and meanwhile, a compulsion in his mind allows him to scratch his whole body for the imaginary worms. Both conditions are very much irritable. The itch irritates the person who has itch. The person who harbours external zoopathy irritates all his family members.

"Doctor, how do you define 'irritability'? My college-going boy is irritable. I find it difficult to control him."

You are right because he is irritable; he is not irritable to his neighbours. He is irritable to you and to your wife. You have no daughter; if you have one she is also irritable. Children are irritable to their parents so also parents are irritable to their children. This is a universal phenomenon. There is always a gap or space existing in which age, experience and expectations do not fit comfortably. All these three never mix totally but I see only emulsification as, as a chemistry professor puts it. This emulsification is an illusion because solution appears mixed but under microscope they are not. Hence, at any time this emulsified mixture can be separated to their original states. Here this solution is not made up of sugar, salt and water. This is exactly what I would like to tell you. For a young couple having a child is like sugar, when the child grows up you keep experiencing a pinch of salt and the money you hoard is for your children to spend like water. Therefore in life sugar, salt and water though appear separate but fused beyond separation. Do not take my statement at its face value but try to meditate on my statement. Invariably, the bondage we keep talking are not true bondages but they are relative bondages. If my friend says that he lives without money, he is a big liar. There is no logic behind these statements. I have seen people getting their children married and keep posing as my duty is over, but what about their responsibility. You are the witness to your responsibility until your end. This responsibility ends when you die. In this journey, somewhere in your mind your expectations on family members pinches you; an expectation in my brain that my son is not like me, and an expectation in my heart that my daughter is not like my wife. These expectations are out of love and affections because of the gene bondage but not out of shared bondages. I have seen families where father dying does not hurt his son but when his dog dies it hurts him more. These shared bondages are lethal and are more painful. This is what happens in our society. The shared bondages in religion have turned into exploding bombs. The religion has divided our country. Blasphemy is a tool to destroy the ethos of the society. When ethos of the society is at jeopardy, the morality disintegrates and the silent social anarchy eats away the fruit of harmony. This is all because of the deep relative bondages with Gods created by innumerable religions. People have forgotten the one and the only religion called as the "religion of humanity." Hence, my dear friend, the shared bondages are lethal only when the religion is attacked but in the case of bondage with gene seen, this is never the issue. Here, religion does not exist because only egos exist. It is the ego of father over his son and the ego of his son over the father. This silent drama in a nuclear family can be witnessed and felt only by their actors. This is not a staged drama, whereas religious dramas played are all premeditated and with certain intensions and expectations. These staged dramas could be felt by all. How? Politicians could feel the gain, religious heads could feel the power and the common man like you and I could feel the loss. Here ego does not play, it is the muscle, money and power help but in a nuclear family it is the love and hate relationship, which matters most for an "irritability." It is the expectation by father, which hurts his son, and it is the liberty of his son, which hurts him so bad. When I hurt you, you get angry. The expression of this anger leads to aggression and those who watch this *Tamaasha* get irritated. Irritation is a mindset because the mind is preset most of the times with "obsessions." These obsessions do not allow any time for the son to think about what father advices and for father about what the son wants out of him. Those who are irritable do not lose their hearts but those who have fear lose their hearts. Hence, it is good to possess irritability rather than to harbour fear. But invariably, both present simultaneously for their love's sake. Because he is his son, she is his daughter and she is his wife. When this relationship crops the hierarchy does popup. In hierarchy, the ego never shuns but brightens up, so automatically the "irritability." Hence, Lord Buddha asked irrespective of relationship to be friends but this never happens in a family for the simple reason that son never shares alcohol with his father and daughter never shares in a mother's kitty party. Hence, "Irritability" is a universal phenomenon. Do not try to read a psychiatry textbook for the cause of "irritability" because you never understand the words these authors uses.

When this is the real nature of "irritability," what could be a possible remedy to this? The remedy could be my Open Meditation. Listen carefully, you said your son is "irritable";

do not find any clarification from any psychiatry textbooks, because there are many theories which confuse the layman. Neuro-scientists explain irritability as secondary to neural looping problem. I explain the same in a gist. The signals we perceive do not reach the area in brain, which is meant for this particular signal. Hence, this signal never reaches its centre. Therefore, the signal takes short route and behaves like a short circuit. We all know that what effect this short circuit would cause in our homes. Similarly, in our brain, this short circuit expresses itself in the form of irritability. For our convenience, our anger is the expression of irritable mind. As I have already said that this irritable nature of a person is like a strong itch and in this itch the person would experience numb, which scuttles the incoming interferences and disturbances as he keeps on scratching. He would have lost his senses to the outer world and also to his inner world. This would lead to lack of reasoning in him.

Have you watched your son when he was is in an irritable mood? You would have seen him irritable when you have not fulfilled his itch of owning a bike, not allowing him to get a mobile, asking him to hand over his mobile, inquiring his whereabouts when he had bunked his classes, when enquired about his habits, etc. His gesture appears like a snarling monkey. Thank God, our canines and our nails are rudimentary.

After all, mood and affect are the two facets of emotion, the emotion is expression of motion. Frankly, it is not the words that precipitate irritability but it is the gesture or the outburst. It is usual for the son to feel that the father's criticism is responsible for his non-performance. It is usual for the father to feel that his *Karma* or some curse is the reason behind his son's shortfall. Invariably, failure in finding the aptitude of their children is the root cause for our children's failure. If in a family with gene bondages, the advice, the acceptance, the motivational curse, the encouraging criticism are not addressed or viewed properly, then there will begin a war called as Adjustment Reaction. In this condition, one would see real irritation and irritability. Viewing and addressing the said attributes depend on the genes expressional quality with along other psycho-social, economic and environmental factors. As a responsible father, he should reduce criticising his son and as a responsible son he should accept the curse from his father as curative. If these two "life" attributes are at jeopardy, it bequeaths unpleasant sounds.

Coming to the point of irritation, for your irritation, the irritating factor could be your son's irritability. This saga continues as long as the *Samsara* remains in this world. This irritability stops as soon as the gene hierarchical bondage stops. This is the time when all of us are liberated or feel freedom and start feeling as one family (*Vasudeva Kutumbam*). Let me pray, this statement of mine could be a prelude to good in future.

For us, each passing day is a transitional phase from traditional and cultural values to changing biological and technological savvy we are facing in this competitive world. The inherited morality and learnt ethos are like sugarcanes passing through sugarcane crushing machine. From each turn of the crusher, the sugarcane of morality and ethos are getting squeezed and on the other side sweet remains as sweet but without much strength, which is necessary to hold the life bricks tight. Because of this reason, our virtues are decimating fast. When our esteemed value systems are being beaten to the changing trends of human liberalism, the word "irritability" does find a firm place in our life treasury. As long as this irritability holds a place in our mind, the anger prevails. The expressed part of irritability is anger or emotional outburst and non-expressive part of the same irritability is dejection and despair. Too much of anger would lead to disastrous problems in the given context and the dejection leads to frustration, which is a non-contextual thing leading to depression and suicide. Anger is momentary; hence, an affective disorder, but the frustration is not momentary, which prevails inside our psyche for longer duration and hence a mood disorder. An impulsive anger could have criminal implications of self-harm or harm to others, but frustration would require awareness, high attention, good observation, better reasoning and more understanding. This you cannot practice with your closed eyes but this is a possibility only when you meditate with your eyes open. This is how my Open Meditation helps to manage our irritability. Irrespective of the age, it is the knowledge accreditation, which helps the person to outsmart our despairs and dysphoria. I do not ask you to read Mahabharata or Ramayana, but focus on the daily life page from the mammoth scripture Jeeva Darshana (practical encyclopaedia of life behavior). Your PhD's, double degree or MBBS does not help to understand the life better but minimum observation of life events and finding maximum reasons to the same would do much to this wayward society. My monk, Mouna Muni (Lord of Silence) had said, "A small smile, a frill of good gesture, a pat from heart, tiny exchange of pleasantries and a fine aroma of trust converts this world into Heaven." Can you do all these things with your closed eyes? It is impossible; these life attributes would require eyes wide open. This is exactly how my Open

Meditation helps in managing many nuisances in our mind. I remember to have read Socrates caged and chained before his execution who had answered a wise man, "Honestly, my greatest moments were 'arguments' in my life," for the question "Which were the greatest moments in your life?" He also had answered this wise man about his last wish "My last wish is I would love to die again." The moral of these two statements is that arguments within a living gene–social bondage should be viewed as curative. The member who wanted to be wise in an argumentative situation would keep the curse and so also the criticism at bay. For all our suicidal feelings and behavior or self-harm attitude, we should try to understand Socrates wish because what we leave in this earth is meagre knowledge and to improve on this knowledge and faith in himself he should wish for frequent deaths. The same principle Maha Rushi Pathanjali had explained in his dossiers to increase the cumulative refined *Karma* from one generation to another generation. This theory exactly fits in to the Hindu Philosophy, which explains the doctrine of Reincarnation.

Your question was how best my Open Meditation would help in preventing irritation of mind or "irritability." Very simple, you feel the pulse of your son's wanting. He wants a bike, get it and his irritability vanishes but along with the bike you buy fear. From fear, you are allowing your heart to function minimal and he finds the thrill from the speed the bike generates. You have to read on Betting and Gambling in my second English book Paavithratha (the life). I have explained the thrill in this chapter. Hence, fear and irritability always are like a railway tracks. They neither converge nor break away. Hence, there is nothing in the world or in our mindset that we are free from, fear, anger, worry, sorrow, dull, boredom, irritable and depression. All these attributes are like *Kauruvas* of *Kuru's* dynasty. We have to learn to live along with these disturbing people and find a mechanism of diplomacy beforehand to comply with the causes for irritation in our life. Once you find the cause, you are able to find a possible answer for the cause you have in front of you or try to solve the cause in question from the available resources around you. This is exactly the "Intelligence" or near to what my Open Meditation meant. Intelligence is a British word, whereas my Open Meditation is a *Desi* (local language) word, the one and only difference is that mixing of my consciousness with the consciousness of another person while interacting beforehand. The Mixing part is otherwise called as Yoga. So, according to me the Intelligence and the Yoga when both prevail at one point and solve the problem in question effectively is called more precisely as Open Meditation. Confusing, listen now carefully—

The first step would be that you try to understand your son's skill of riding a bike. Could his age permit for the license to drive the bike or not. Explain to your son the pros and cons of different types of bikes after educating him the purpose of buying a bike. Explain the recurrent expenditure his vehicle would require. Find out your source of income etc. Here we have to meditate on two paths, risk path and skill path. You are the judge to both paths, but as there are no lawyers representing both these paths, you fail in your Judgment. And then, with all the explanations that you have provided to your son if nothing works then you buy a bike to your son's choice and wait for the fear. If this is the theory then listen to this story of a monk. Once my Mouna Muni was asked a question by one of his disciples,

"O enlightened master, tell me how your silence helps my meditation," monk said, "It never helps you." "Why the hell should I practice my silence then if there is no gain from meditation," monk said, "Yes I did not gain anything; it is a loss for me practicing silence." The furious disciple was about to open his mouth, but the ever-smiling monk said, "Wait, listen what did I loose, I lost fear, irritability, anger, boredom, dejection, despair, hate, doubts, greed, depression and so on." Suddenly, the disciple fell to Mouna Muni's feet and got relieved of his innocence. Hence, I advise you to follow the Mouna Muni even after you get your son a race bike. From the time you purchase a bike to your son, by meditating, you notice two things, your son could become a racer or get admitted to a hospital.

"Doctor is it inevitable to buy a bike for my son?"

"Definitely, it is not just a bike; you should buy him a mobile, after getting him a mobile, you have to buy an internet pack, if he has a separate room at your home, you also should buy him a television with some loaded sky pack. With all these gadgets and total submission to your son, probably he would find a lover of his choice, not of your choice. Machine gadgets are yours and life gadget is his. After his marriage, you are just a mute spectator inviting *Chira Nidhra* (eternal sleep). I do not say it is so with all, but in majority of them. We do find good children, you see."

FAMILY AND OPEN MEDITATION"

"Doctor, tell us how Open Meditation of yours helps in a family setting."

Exactly, today we have to set the family in order. Today, the scenario of family norms is losing its luster. When the eastern tradition is getting snubbed by the onslaught of western culture, the families have been fragmented. Today the strength of the family bricks are vanishing fast. Hence, as days progress, the unit of family has to be seen under microscope. We may fail in our venture in bringing our families because today the matrimonial expectations are going wayward and skyward. Recently, there was an advertisement in an matrimonial column in which the girl's wish about her hubby was, "I am a tom boy—he has to bear with me, I do not grow my hair long—he should accept me, I do not like a child—he should comply with this, I hate my parents because they pester me to marry a boy of their choice—hence, he should hate my parents, I like a person who would take his own decisions and be very independent of me, he should not try to have a control on me" and so on and so forth. Now, you tell me, what would be the traditional, cultural and customary values of such marriages. In a marriage set-up, there are few quotients one has to look into, they are—the "societal role adaptations, family role adaptations and mutual role adaptations." When this trilogy works within the framework of obligations, the setting up of a family is easy. The previously mentioned quotients when keep increasing with the given psycho-socio-economic quadrants, the bondage in the family grips well with the given space and time. It is true that as our world is dynamic not static, the families too have found different trends but still families have not completely been ruined. Hence, all is not bad; still we can set the family with repeated knowledge imposition of family norms to our young. At this juncture, I have to tell you a story—recently, I had come across a couple. Her chief complaint was headache. She was in-between the forty-five to fifty age group. She was having two grown-up children who were studying in boarding college. I presume that her husband is having adult ADHD. He drives his car at a speed of one hundred and fifty km per hour, never sits at one place and he would engage himself for eight to ten hours to his mobile. Against his first wife's wish, he had married for the second time. He does not listen to his children's advice. He has megalo-manic attitude to his first wife that he had given all the material to her and expects to listen to whatever he does, outside and inside. He expects her to remain in a golden cage with her wings folded. He is a high-striving man and had reached a top position in his chain-linked business. His wife should not question him, if she does the same, he is Mohamed Ali to her, if she pursues, he would be Bruce Lee to her, that is, he would physically harass and abuse her. When he had been brought to me, one could physically sense the sub-scapular hematomas (small encapsulated blood collection between the scalp and the skull). This time, he had brought her to me for the guilt of punishing her. After further examination, she had numerous bruises all over and soft tissue injuries secondary to the chair he had used against her. The reason for this state would be that she raised her voice against his desires. He justifies his punishment for her nagging attitude. He had brought her to me with advice that she should not speak to any one because that would jeopardize his business. He was habituated to alcohol and smoking. The blunt injuries were so severe that she was passing myoglobinurea (muscle protein in her urine). One day, she just slipped out from her locked home to her native place without her husband's knowledge after a tip-off to her brother.

Look into this family, material is there but mutual trust has gone into the gutter. Now what would you call to this anomaly? Is it our changing value system? Is it our cultural morality to be rich and famous, not love? Is it that we are following western copycats? I was shocked to know that a youth convict having some mind aberration giving an interview inside the jail to a foreign anchor airing his view about the woman whom he raped, to accept his advances. His argument was about the victim's dress code and the timing to which she was engaged to a boy (party and pub). My advice for this moral maroon is that why he would have not advised her to go home or he could have escorted to her home. Why was she raped and killed? Yes, there also lay societal obligations to our women and girls. Imposing moral of conduct to our women is against their human rights but this code of conduct should be taught as a lesson to our children so that we presume that probable future problems could be averted. It is left to the individuals to follow morality or not, because as long as people are immoral how can they speak against immorality.

MORALITY

"Doctor, you kept on using the adjective 'morality', how does it help people at large?"

Morality is one subject that could not be taught so easily in our schools; earlier as students, we had moral stories to imbibe morality. Now it has taken a beating, crushed and vanquished from the educationist's dictionary. It is presumed that morality in our orthodox society would get transmitted through the genes. Hence, morality does not enter our mind forcefully. We take for granted that morality already exists in our psyche. It is a myth. This morality subject is a tough subject to learn, and if we learn this morality, we do not survive in this society. If you want to do your business, you should keep morality at little distance, it does not mean that you should forget morality in total. This is a accepted norm of any business society. Total immorality is forbidden in the society. Therefore, in this dichotomy, definitely you ask me about the *Laksham Rekha* between morality and immorality. For this, I do not have absolute answers but I can find it via an answer. I would answer in very simple words that it is for you to choose what is morality and immorality. The answer is like psychiatrists perspective of a psychiatric condition. Two psychiatrists disapprove common finding, as it is prerogative thinking of two learned consciousness. In other words, approval of symptom is secondary to their subjective interpretations. Morality is like psychiatry, which is purely subjective approach. Today, psychiatry is no more a subjective study because the psychiatric nomenclature should suit the Indian Classification of Diseases or Diagnostic Statistical Manual (DSM-5). Hence, psychiatry is more science oriented but not the morality. Morality is philosophical. We speak moral science but this subject lacks the evidence-based proof for what is moral and what is immoral. This is why I call "Creator created consciousness." Hence, moral science is already present in our genes or transmitted as one among many mind functions of a person from generation to generation. According to Patanjali, this gene could be thawed or kindled to encrypt bad or the good. For a software in computer, the engineer's learnt consciousness is a source for coding, similarly coding for the morality is our own consciousness through self-engineer program, which could be stored so that good moral standards are transmitted to our next generation.

I will give one simple example for this. I had been to a family get-together. In our Hindu culture, it is customary for the head of the family to offer "rice" ritually (*Bhaagina* in Kannada language) to his daughters. This was done in a grand scale by my wife's uncle. The function was well attended by his relatives. I have a habit of taking an afternoon nap. The only room having a bed to nap was occupied by relative children aged between eight to twelve years. While I was resting with my closed eyes, the children thought that I was sleeping, but in fact I was awake and I was curious to know what play they are going to play. It was amazing to know their standard of English with broken local language Kannada. This was the time I remembered politicians and literates double speak on our local language. Though these children had come from the city, it is the wish of their parents to master English for their children. Similarly, the politicians and local language literates speak importance of their local language Kannada. Meanwhile, imposition of Kannada legally in all schools and brandishing their mite towards non-Kannada talking people is not acceptable. It is irony that these set of people send their children to English convent schools. Hence, I have no issue if a child speaks English, but I made my children compulsory to study the local language Kannada till their seventh standard because i love my local language Kannada.

The play these children were playing was King and Queen. It is interesting to find that the twelve year old was a female child and the play played was around Queen. If it were to be other way in terms of sex, it was a King's play. This play was not their original idea but was asked to be played in their schools by their teachers or presumably there could be a play in their curriculum. Why I am making my point on this is that the play was almost natural, it was like a professional drama. All others below her age were soldiers or subordinates and have to follow what the Queen orders. Probably, I was lying down for almost an hour. To my amaze, their play never found any role for Rama, Sitha or Krishna. The play was more of a western type. It is unfortunate that we do not have any space for our heroes who fought against all odd to snatch back our freedom from them. Their effort was commendable, heroic and altruistic. We have in front of us many moral stories but we fail in putting these stories in our primary curriculum. What I could understand from their play was only to command and to get the things done like "Bring luggage, take luggage to room, be careful about the luggage," any problem while following these orders, "Prepare for severe punishment." Hence, the whole play was Order and Punishment.

Now we speak of *Chote Chote Baathse Hamara Parivarthan Hoga Aur Rashtreke Vikas Hoga.* This is exactly what I would like to teach you, if you want your custom, tradition, culture and religion to stay, it is only small things that help not big things. For example, if this eldest female child had taken the role of Seetha, one could find different mindsets altogether when they grow old. Hence, impart our epic stories in the primary curriculum so that King and Queen would be forgotten and only Rama, Seetha and Krishna would be remembered for the generations to come in our country. Likewise, there are many moral stories across the world but it does not mean that we should forget our great epics. I hope you do not give any political colour to my statement. The moral science of all my explanation to you is that how best our tradition, our culture, our customs and our religion could find an inscription in our genes? Simple, if the play played by the young children had taken the role of Seetha by the eldest girl, Laxmana, Nakula, Bharatha and Hanumantha by other artistes' could change the mindset in these youngsters. How? Seetha had never ordered Rama to kill Ravana. Rama killed only evil. Hence, in this way, our customs continue forever with the young alike. I hope you followed by technique of Open Meditation in this subject.

I will tell you another interesting story. Our mindset by default or by birth is programmed for shining objects. Gold is one example. Lord Buddha does shine, but this shine is not like gold, hence nobody goes in search of Lord Buddha. Similarly, we are tuned ourselves for good looks. We tend to marry good-looking girls. One of my many rich friends had married to an ultra-good-looking girl. He got married rapturously amidst fanfare. I could not attend his marriage, as the marriage was held at a far off distant place. He was always intending to marry a good-looking girl; after a few years, I met him. He was dull and dejected. The reason for his dejection really baffled me. He said, "Look Nagesh, I have developed of late aversion towards my wife." "Why? You wanted a smart looking girl." "No, it is not the issue." "What is the issue?" "I cannot explain." "You have to explain, otherwise how will I come to know, is it her behavior, is it her adjustment problem, is it problems with your parents, is it she demands more money as pocket money, is it she does not cook for you, does she have any illness, common, you should explain?" With lots of persuasion, I could find the exact reason why she was not liked by him. It was not her smile but her laugh that was the culprit as it has the quality of prosodynia. He said, "When she laughs, her laugh irritates me because when she laughs she sounds to me as a crow, you know I hate crows." Suddenly, it flashed me; he is suffering from misophonia (highly irritable to a particular sound) to the sounds of crow calls. When his wife laughs he shuts his eyes and closes his ears. If she is not laughing, he is absolutely fine with her. But the problem with her is that she never smiles, she always laughs. This is the problem in him, and his repeated advice went into her deaf ears. He consulted many ENT surgeons and speech pathologists, but his venture in correcting her high pitch shrill laughs could not be corrected. This continued almost for two years of their marriage. This had left a vacuum in their married life towards a probable separation. He wanted a solution from me because he knew that I practice Open Meditation. I asked him, "Who taught you to close your eyes and cover your ears when she laughs?" "Yes, I attended many meditation classes to cool myself from the irritation, one *Guru* taught me this technique from the irritation she produces." This is exactly what happens with meditation with closed yes. I told him, "Stop the previous technique and tune your wife to close her mouth with her hands whenever she intends to laugh or while laughing by a look of yours eyes wide open." This worked for him; this is exactly my Open Meditation is all about. If he had closed his eyes for each of her laughs, probably, he might have divorced her in the next few years. Fortunately we met. Until now, probably I assume that he is happy to the technique of my Open Meditation taught to him and I presume he is living happily. This is exactly what my wife practices whenever I talk unwanted things with her or with others; I stop talking immediately to her eyes wide open. Hence, I consider her as my teacher you know.

SATHYA NARAYANA SWAMY

"Doctor, in this present twenty-first century, the *Swamy* concept still prevails. I am confused, could you explain?"

Why not, definitely yes. Let me take an example of Narayana Swamy. Though I am not a surgeon, I dissect these nouns smartly only to find what these nouns stand for. When I dissect this noun I find Nara+Yana+Swamy. Traditionally, we all perform *Sathyanarayna Vratha*. In our Hindu Mythology, this God is an icon for whom every one of us is scared of. I have an interesting story for you before I explain the present concept. One of my many *Chota* Politicians had asked me, "Doctor, my High Command asked me to take initiation on *Swathca Bharath*. You know that I know only the means and ways of sticking to my chair but how can I take a Broomstick and clean the roads and passages strewn with garbage, give me some solution?" This cleaning business is an irony at the present context. When my "Bharath" is not in my blood then how *Swatch Bharath* comes to my mind. There is a reason to say this, listen carefully now, I have a friend, a tennis mate who has orthodox type of playing techniques using his racquet grip in an unusual manner and gives an off spin to the ball and generates such speed for which the opponent gets confused. While he plays, I remember Erapalli Prassanna's off spin. At times, the ball was just unplayable. Invariably, he and his partner would win. I came to know the secret of his grip after several years. Apologetic to him I conjectured on him that his forefathers were mason workers who were trained to take the grout and splash on the wall in an off spin style. Hence, his style was not learnt on his own and his style was in his blood. To tell the truth, he never tried to hold the tennis racquet with present contemporary style of grip holding. Therefore, in any society their mindset always comes in blood. In our country, we are good at cleaning our houses but meanwhile good at throwing litters and garbage into public places.

Now, coming back to Sathya Narayana Swamy, I dissected this word in to three. *Nara*(mythological term for man) cannot be a God but he could be a God if you listen what I say. *Yana* is journey in Kannada language. Hence, when *Nara* takes a journey towards *Sathya,* the truth would become a *Swamy*. *Swamy* in *Vedantha* is a master of knower. You can be a *Swamy* if you cannot bear the untruth. In this situation, you could be God-like. As long as we are entangled with this *Maya* (illusion), the word *Swamy is* very farfetched. However, be careful before you meet any *Swamy*…

BIG BANG

"Doctor, what is Big Bang and where are we heading to? I know you are interested in this field too."

You have asked this question to a wrong person, yet I try to answer. Before I answer your question, let me submit my innocence on mathematics and on astronomy, neither a mathematician nor the astronomer. Whatever I have answer for you are from two articles I read recently on the subject "Pi" and what I guess on the contents of recent article "big bang theory." This question is like, what is Pi. To my understanding, this Pi is to find the ratio of a diameter to a circumference of a circle. As this circle is round and round, we are not able to find the true decimal. When everything is within the circle, we failed to evolve the answer. The same analogy holds good for the question you have asked. In your question, there is something" sling. Any object sling thrown has maximum thrust. Hence, speed. I am not sure whether we were spiralled out from the point of explosion or were just pushed out tremendously from the source of explosion. Whatever may be the force by which we are thrown out but one thing is certain is that we are moving. I am not moving as one piece but as a whole solar system is moving; hence, I do not feel that I am moving. I strongly feel that if your sling thrown theory is correct, the behavior in which this universe is acting is correct. Because, each object in this universe have taken a circular tangential path from a distant object, which has phenomenal electromagnetic influence on the said object, which has found a circular path on this particular object. Hence, pushing theory is ruled out. If an astrologist or physicist now proves this pushing theory is true, the push or the speed in which we are travelling would be calculated in even numbers. So, there would not have been Archimedes Pi, because Pi does not possess even decimal. This is exactly the reason why Pi is still interesting to mathematicians. When we are able to find correct decimal to Pi, then we presumably may find a path towards where we are heading to and from where we have thrown the sling or a place from where we are pushed out from the point of explosion that is said to have taken place millions of years back. Our planet smashing with another planet is a remote possibility because all planets move in one direction. This direction could be opposite to the direction of the source of big bang or moving in a circle to a source of our origin. Nothing stops the planets moving. Hence, for all practical purpose, there is no collusion. According to Hindu teachings, if *Kalpa* (contraction and expansion) is a possibility, then there could be only contraction and then expansion. These theories have been described at length by many physicists including Stephen Hawking from their Black Hole existence in space. Even when we are dragged towards these black holes, we do not die or the earth would not get destroyed for the simple reason that we are just trespassing a different hidden universe. Once again, we are ejected out from the explosion that could probably take place beneath the core of such black holes due to the enormous amount of heat produced by the friction they generate from the speed of the mass that would collide at the centre by their astounding power of gravity. What I have narrated here is not to take literally but what I mean here is about our dormant life.

Whatever may be the destruction we face but at the end of the day, there remains an atom of life. It is all theories you know, but if our earth has been thrown with a sling, there is a possibility that our earth could escape the gravity of a black hole as we are able to scrape through tangentially at the Horizon of this particular black hole to which we are attracted. Hence, as this universe is so massive, infinite and so deep, unless we are not able to answer the Pi, we are not able to find where we are heading to.

In our Hindu teachings, whenever there is any material offerings to Brahmin or during any material transactions of our rituals, generally, we tend to offer hundred and one rupees instead of hundred rupees. This behavioral attitude of ours really baffles me. I think probably we all knowingly or unknowingly accept the Pi's existence in our ancient mathematics. Because the true value of Pi is always in odd decimals. To know about your question there is another way of calculating the *Kalpa* of this universe. This calculation is based on *Vipaasa* theory of Lord Buddha or *Shuunya* theory of Aryabhat. By using our present innovative technological tools, if our scientists are able to calculate the existing space around us, probably we are sure of finding a solution to the point of our destination and also from where exactly big bang had occurred. There is also another way of finding the death and birth of this universe, wherein if we are able to compute the magnitude of whole matter of this universe, there could be a possibility of finding birth and death. Hence, as long as we are not able to calculate all these mathematical probabilities in an absolute way, we do not exactly know to where we are heading to and also we are not able to find the point of big bang have had taken place.

BLISS

"Doctor, in your second English book Paavithratha (the attributes of life), you have given lots of importance to "solace." You have mentioned little about "happiness." Would you explain the difference between these two?"

The perfect line between these two attributes of life is difficult to draw. Today, we do not require colleges and universities. All information are available by just paying a few thousands for a laptop with loaded internet pack. Hence, there is no difficulty to have the information regarding many complicated words but to apply the same attributes into reality life with practicality is a difficult proposition. At this point of discussion, let me not go to Wikipedia or Oxford dictionary. Because whatever you are going to coin a new word or if you have a metaphor that is used repeatedly in the public domain, it automatically would find a place in these informative and material dictionaries like today's "selfies." Therefore, my point of contention is that difference between "solace, happiness and bliss" has no much differences. When I talk on "solace," which is a happy state, like which could be given by a person or professional like me. Through my antidepressant prescriptions and by my counselling I could give "solace" to the depressed patient after a material transaction. Happiness is not a value to be given by me because this happiness is a self-related psychological mechanism. This happiness comes within hence cannot be given by any means by any professional or by somebody. The word "bliss" could not be defined. If I say that I have bliss, people tell me that I am suffering from Happy Psychosis. Bliss could be a mood or a schizophrenic disorder. In my first book Parivarthana (the change), I have mentioned about an untreated schizophrenic who was always smiling. For me and you, our achievements or doing well to the society should make us smile. This roadside schizophrenic was shabby, unkempt, sitting along the garbage and eating rotten food still smiling. This is what I call bliss because he was hearing God's voice presumably. If a Yogi talks of bliss, he is a *Dongi* yogi, because he would have achieved this state of bliss after cannabis use.

You too have achieved this bliss state, can you tell me when did you achieve it?

"No, I have not experienced, because neither am I a schizophrenic nor a manic."

Wrong, you have experienced it. Now fall back to a state wherein you are in this situation or you had this state. Go back, you find it.

"No, I am not able to."

No, I ask you to be in a state where you are copulating with your wife. Total bliss is a moment or *Kshana* when you reach your orgasmic state. In this condition, there creates a total void where you are disconnected with the whole world. There are no good or bad thoughts, there are no good or bad ideas and you have mystic experience with least emotions. This is the period where there is derealisation and depersonalisation effect. You do not know who entered your premises. You do not know who is watching you. You have forgotten God is watching you.

You forget whether your spouse is having bliss or not. This bliss state is just an energy you are giving and your spouse is taking. This is exactly a "bliss" state where without your knowledge you are passing on the life from one generation to another generation. If this bliss state was not there, this world would not have been there. It is something centrally deep in our consciousness, so deep no one could penetrate. This state one cannot experience because it is not situated superficially. I have seen people visiting *Manasa Sarovara.* They say that have attained bliss without knowing or finding the mystic lake inside their consciousness. People always would misinterpret serenity with bliss. If humans do not attain bliss, please find that there is no world or God. Hence, the God is so cunning that He has asked us to experience this "bliss" state only during copulation. Please understand if you attain this "bliss state" now, you forget your wife, you forget your children, you forget the God, you forget the world, you forget the food and hence if you ask yourself to live deluded with bliss, you remain alone, you are single, you have no interest, you have no motivation, you do not work so on and so forth. In this state, the world stops moving. When there is no movement in this world, the world is going to end. This is exactly what *Pralaya* means to me. Now tell me my friend, you want this bliss now.

"No Doctor, I would like to experience blissful state for a given chance of moment."

Do not be optimistic my friend, what "bliss" you require is beyond your reach because only few could experience the "bliss" in this world. Albert Einstein obtained his bliss when he invented $E=MC^2$, Newton attained "bliss" when he found the reason for his thrown apple to fall, Martin King Luther and Nelson Mandela attained their "bliss" when they fought for apartheid, Mahatma Gandhi attained "bliss" when he got us independence, Lord Buddha got his "bliss" when he had enlightenment. Likewise, many scientists, sociologists, economists and anthropologists experienced "bliss" when they found reasons and solutions to uplift the human sufferings. Hence, this "bliss" is central, which is all-pervading. From this statement, you should know that this "bliss" is not to keep, "bliss" from great people was there to spread to the hedonist society and obtained "bliss" should be there to share among all living beings.

Sometimes "bliss" has been confused with ecstasy. Ecstasy is state of ultimate euphoria. Euphoric are maniacs and megalomaniacs. Invariably, "euphoria" and "ecstasy" do not present with so-called normal individuals. This ecstasy is present with those who consume LSD, cocaine, morphine and heroin. To tell you the truth, ignorant and innocent individuals could possess this "bliss," like a farmer who experience "bliss" after doing his hard work in the day and getting his good sleep at night. This farmer could share his enriched "bliss" as an end product (food) to millions of people around him. After utilising his grains and vegetables, it could be a further "bliss" to the fellow population who always depend on such "bliss" as food. Bliss could be seen with a person who shares his food among starved individuals in spite of his hungry. Bliss could be seen with a professional like a doctor who could give a life in spite of his many hurdles (in cases of natural calamities a surgeon operated on thirty to forty patients a day to give back their lives). Bliss could be seen with a social worker who does relentless service to humankind in spite of his family sufferings. Bliss could be seen with a scientist who does wonders to society through his inventions in spite of his personal sufferings. The list goes on and on like a kite tail but at end of the day we keep jumping, hoping and leaping to have a "bliss," which is very easy to possess the "alcohol."

This exactly what my Open Meditation preaches. I teach you to arouse yourself to experience the probable instant "bliss" you could come across, I ask you to arrive for possible conclusions from the "bliss" you experience and you activate your consciousness to the intended "bliss" you just experienced to merge the same in the time and to spread the experience you experienced in the space around you.

MOUNA MUNI

"Doctor, always you mention on Mouna Muni, who is this *Muni*?"

It is a good inquisitive question, dear. Before I explain this great man, I would like to explain something to you. Hearing presumably would allow you to open your eyes wide. Hence, my explanation could be a prelude to my Open Meditation. The forgotten philosophers always stuck to their point of Art when education was considered by them. Mere education like British education system (which we follow in our curriculum) would go to the drains, if the student's "self" is not carved out from his masters towards a perfect Art. The present educational standard is more of a stereotypical *Makki Ka Makki* (mere copy) type. They believe in books rather than in lifestyle. Human is basically a living palaeographic structure embedded with mystique consciousness. In temples, we worship non-moving icons blessed with beautiful carvings. The carved designs on these Gods and Goddess would have probably left with obsessions for the viewers depending on their oestrogen and testosterone levels. This is the reason why I exactly stick to Art. Individual in his own capacity is a building block to the present society. Each individual in this world is been designed in a copycat style. Creator has gifted consciousness individually, which are different in its functional and expressive capacity. Moving man cannot be designed further. This could be a possibility from a plastic surgeon. Hence, man could only be groomed. From his early evolutional phase, he was devoid of humane attributes. From generations to generations, the philosophical approach by the then philosophers to create Humanity has made their attempt to chip of the unwanted part of each individual's corner stone to make a perfect present state of human. This is done not on human's body but they did it on their mind. No matter what this part of art is actually has allowed man to adopt or to assume how he is in a place to come out from the difficulties he faced or going to face. This art of making been termed as "intelligence" by the so-called the intelligentsia of now.

Generally, the intelligentsias of the present world are divided among themselves as professors, masters and spiritualists. My education has allowed me to become only doctor. After several years of practice and understanding the mundane, I thought of changing my profession proverbially. However, unlike in the west, in the east after confirmation of your first degree, you cannot change the same degree to another degree legally. Hence, whatever we find today degrees on spiritualism, which are conferred on spiritualists (anybody can become spiritualist) are self-made certificates. Basically, people in this country believe on *Deeksha* conferred on to a student *Sanyasi* from senior *Sanyasi* or *Guru*. For your today's spiritualism, you need not have to go to a known university, which preaches only on spiritualism and confers a degree on the spiritualism. You might be having a degree in *Vedanta* but not in spiritualism. Hence, for all practical purposes today, the spiritualists to whom we come across are self-made spiritualists and are self-made godmen. When I was left with the term Doctor permanently in my consciousness, I was restless several times for a selfish motive, "why I had not became a professor." Today's profession of mine as doctor is only by chance. This story been explained in length in my second Kannada book Manassu Mrudanga. As I always conjure on my work mainly on certain hypothesis, hence I divided my consciousness into four parts. I kept profession as one-quarter but my other three-quarters as Professor, Literate and Spiritualist. In my second Kannada book, you have my detailed picture of three-quarters of me as a psychiatrist, as a professor and as a literate but you do not find the last quarter of mine as spiritualist. Hence, I am privileged to explain who this Mouna Muni is.

As this mute materialistic world is changing, the life on earth feels the heat and brunt of its survival. The life could be anything. It could be the virus to humans. From the invention of new antiviral to expensive bactericidal drugs, the virus and bacteria would sketch themselves for their survival in the form of mutation so that they could adapt to the invented new drugs for their survival. The biological patterns of man never alter or change to the psycho-social mutations of this world to survive, because man would always try to adapt consciously or unconsciously to the changing patterns of this world of materialism. The changing pattern would be the confusion he is living in, the educational standards we set, the incomplete medical profession we render, the competition man encounters, the constraints of individuals' financial system, the meanness of people around him, the man and animal conflict he is in, the present political system man is facing, the ill-defined religions he belongs to, the frequent changing legislations on caste and creed, the interactive psychological turmoil we face, the socio-economical standards we are in, the failing present-day relationships, the incomplete coping mechanisms we learn, the liberalized attitude of the either sex, the egos of either sex, the falling quality in the working places, the recent influx of corporate business, the social ills of the society, the huge lacuna we have created with innumerable language, the changing perspective of religious conversions, the natural disasters we face, the incomplete security we are provided with, the growing population in this world, the joblessness thus created, the socio-economic inequality in this world, the fear of nuclear arms this world possesses, the terrorists we are nurturing, the unplanned growth of our cities, the heat of changing technologies, the changing medico-legal systems in this world, the legal dichotomies the man is exposed to, the double talk of the world leaders, the meagre support system to our scientists, etc.; for all these parameters, man has succumbed to despair out of understandable fear. Automatically, with all perplexities of life, man has succumbed to various psychological complexities that need urgently various mechanisms to take away the fear in this man. In the medieval time, man was haphazardly vulnerable to animals and enemies, and thus for his survival, he was running and hiding from being killed. Now he has all the living capabilities with material and money but he is not happy, leave alone solace in him because his mind is confused, he is fearful and he is non-directive to a given solution. Hence, he requires instantly a mechanism to cool his hot heels so that his mind would calm down a bit. The available mechanism today is counselling. In this counselling, there are two types. One is from professional side and another is from spiritual side. Under the given circumstances, the professionalism has not got sharp tools to counsel as this branch lacks the quality of conveying and convincing because this system purely based on science. The branch of spiritualism does not ask any degree or university recognition, because this branch relies mainly on bogus propaganda. As media drives this branch through their haired *Swamies* with their colourful talks or discourses for which people simply fall prey to these illogical pseudo-stalwarts. This is for the simple reason that the science I talk has of no role here, as this science would not show any thing subjectively and substantially. Today, people feel that magic is a miracle. The true miracle is just a change from what they are through counselling. If this statement is true, then what counselling is?

"Counselling is a process in which a skilled learned man would impart his cognizance of skill to a troubled man in order to come out from the troubles he has."

This does not mean that the learned man would render his money to the person who has no money or he would share his wife to a person who does not possess a wife. This counselling technique is a simple commonsense art of delivery system by a professional or learned man to a confused man in which he would advise to use a person's available resources around him to overcome his difficulties. It is seen that in any psychological breakdown or in any physical disasters in the form of natural calamities, people would be in a state of shock, grief and dejection. Adding to his harsh problems possibly, he would suffer from "derealisation" and "depersonalisation." In this condition, what this suffered man would actually need is warmth, sympathy and empathy. These things could be provided by any person who has humane tendency in him and not necessarily a learned man or a so-called the God man.

This "Godman" is a recent trend in our society. In my thirty-two years of experience, I have become God to my patients when I lifted their depression with suicidal tendency just like a surgeon who would have given a fresh lease of life for a person who suffered life-threatening cancer. To add on to this, many good counsellors have prevented innumerable suicides. To mention few examples, a good friend, a responsible father, a teaching mother, a knowledgeable teacher or any professional man. For a man in trouble, an empathetic neighbour is a God. In these conditions, spirituality does not help. It is the spirit of a person that helps. The study of this spirit is "spirituality," which I have defined and explained in my first official English book Parivarthana (the change) under the chapter Spirituality At Its True Sense. Hence, "spirituality" always stands for the truth. After considering my hypothesis, if a person proclaims as Spiritual Guru is merely a con man. According to me, the "spiritualist" is one who knows *Brahman.* When this *Brahman* is infinite, then how anybody could be called as spiritualist. At this present context, for our convenience, this Spiritualist is one who has more knowledge. This knowledge is not mere scientific knowledge but the knowledge of humbleness, knowledge of initiation of peace, knowledge of social programming, knowledge of accommodation to the needy, knowledge of planning to certain sect who is devoid of such human necessities and knowledge of elaborative psycho-social needs to the people devoid of human touch.

In my school days, I had a friend an intelligent and from an orthodox Hindu poor big brahmin family. We were close and if my remembrance is correct, we were competing for the high marks in science at our class exams. He was an active RSS member and was arrested during emergency period. That was the time I met him with other great leaders who were arrested along with him. I was not an active worker in this organization because I did not like the dictatorial attitude of the RSS seniors with whom I had an experience in one of the camps near my native. I had reached certain posts in this organization in my native, and after this incidence, I said good-bye to RSS. No doubt, that this organization had imparted me *Desha Bhakthi* (patriotism). I am also sure that this organization taught me Chandra Shekhar Azad, Sukdev, Bhagath Singh and Subhash Chandra Bose for my nationalism. This organization had also taught me Inclusive Teachings and not the Excluding Teachings. I would leave to you to think what I am after explaining this organization. I do not know whether it was my friend's fortune or not, he was taught Yoga by one of his RSS jail mate who is no more today, he became a Yoga teacher. This Yoga became a profession to my friend as he had left engineering course in the middle due to his arrest. He had travelled all over the world teaching Yoga and now living a very simple life. He had purchased few acres of land, rearing cows and teaching dance by his wife.

After reading a little of the Upanishath, Pathanjali and Puranas, I tucked his persona to one among my four-quarters of my consciousness to become Mouna Muni. I felt many times unconsciously why I could not become one Yoga *Guru* like him. But his state is beyond my imagination. Hence, what I could do is that I just enjoy oblivious to his persona. I can only conjecture and conjure the Yoga and Spirituality here. I would like to brief now what my Mouna Muni would mean to you. Before that,

The man is funny, whereas as animal is not funny because animal would die as an animal but not this man because every neighbour or men known to him wants him to die as human. Majority of us do die as men not as humans. In finding humanity by a man is a cumbersome procedure. Man always finds easy way to escape from the hard reality, hence to search knowledge he would never try to or make an effort to find where the knowledge is. Unconsciously man always craves for achievements in terms of material and knowledge. To stack or amass material one need not go after knowledge, but to seek this knowledge the man has to go behind learned professionals. This is exactly the reason why our education is so expensive. As these universities are so expensive for me to pay and study, I felt that I would rather try to know the same knowledge sitting alone in the house. While at home alone, I never felt that I am lonely. It is for you to believe or not to believe. I divided my consciousness in to four parts factiously and named each quarter. One-quarter I named after my profession run by accidental Dr Huchurao who got metamorphosed from Dr Ramrao. Another quarter I named after literate Kavi Raju who accidentally by an issue became Kavi Thimma. Third-quarter I named after Prof Nirvaan, who was actually Prof Niranjan. There is a reason why he became Nirvaan from Niranjan. He was made to attain *Nirvaana* by his own students. The detailed explanations for this you have to go through my second Kannada book Manassu Mrudanga. If you do not have access to my book, I briefly explain you about these three mystic people. Dr Ramrao was a psychiatrist like me who was straight, strict and little truth oriented. Because of these three attitudes of his, he was renamed by his own colleagues as Dr Huchu Rao. A doctor friend of his, when enquired about his twisted name, this psychiatrist had burst out with laughter and explained the reason why he was called in this name. In his early professional practicing days, one afternoon he had come across a degree student. This patient was disappointed because this Dr Ramrao was serious and tight-lipped. Probably, this degree student would have had a thought in his mind that all psychiatrists would be more smiling, talking and cracking jokes. This student was under the impression that a psychiatrist should act like a psychiatric patient to know the depth of patient's consciousness so as to empathize him better. This student was also harbouring his own impression that, this sort of psychiatric care is the Uno care of psychiatric patients after he had watched just released Kannada movie in which the psychiatrist was acting like a joker to understand his psychiatric patient better. When this story had shared between his fellow professionals, they too had shared his laugh and next day they morphed his name as Dr Huchu Rao.

Sri Kavi Thimma too has a story. His name was Kavi Raj. After an incidence in his college days, he had a name as *Thimma* (Monkey) instead of *Raja* (king). He was boisterous in his character, drubbed by his classmates, not adjusting and is very independent of his thinking. He was a small literate who never speaks but puts his thoughts in writing. His writing was more philosophical and not on any relationships hence his colleagues, seniors and teachers were not ready to accept. In one of his college day's celebrations, his friend, who was also a literate, presented his *Kavana* (poem) and got the prize. To his surprise, he too had presented beautiful poem san recognition. Later he found that this friend had taken the help of his senior lecture and managed to bag the prize. This incidence raked him, and on the corridor of his college, he picked up quarrel with this friend on a trivial reason who had bagged the prize. For the onlookers, Kavi Raj's behavior was unacceptable and they termed him as Kavi Thimma.

Prof Niranjan was a different kind who is more knowledgeable and had possessed social equations at his fingertips. He was a kind more compassionate, accommodative and adjustable and was having no agenda in his mind to make any fame except to impart goodness to his students. He was unattractive and not good at speaking English. While in his class, he was speaking fluent English in his subject with pin-drop silence all over. In this way, all liked him. He was an asset to his university. He never closed his living quarters because he kept his house as library for his students. He had not compromised in purchasing books as he was married only to the books. Lived simple, ate simple food and spent his earnings simply to books. His campus house would see lock when he was out of station. Two enthusiastic newly admitted boys who knew this professor little had known by their seniors that he would never lock his cupboards and trunks, one night ventured an entry to his quarters from back door as they knew back door is weak and broken which would reflect the government establishments. In their path of their entry to his house, they had come across sub-noxious *Kopina* (undergarments) hanging. Hence, they did their venture by closing their nostrils while entering and while emerging out from the quarters. After entering to his quarters, they could not get any valuables except for the priceless books. They returned empty handed. When Prof returned he welcomed by a write up on the board "Welcome Prof Nirvaan." Next day, he was famous as Prof Nirvaan instead of Prof Niranjan.

Now I tell you who actually this Mouna Muni is, who has all together a different story. This man is highly attractive, had beautiful beard, fair with blue eyes and knew the art of teaching *Yoga Asana.* He never worked or taught Yoga with malicious money-making corporate mind. He had attracted by many followers including good-looking woman. Many wealthy men had approached him and they lured him to open an ashram. He knew the consequences of having ashram with attractive women. He was highly spiritual and never acclaimed miracles to any person or gave instant cures to any man seeking medical assistance. His strategy was to teach only good to people. As days progressed, he was haunted and plagued by many followers, which are hindrances to his spiritual thinking. He decided that it is good to be Mouny for his final high spiritual reach. Without informing or telling, he disappeared to deep wood where now working as a peasant farmer. This is exactly the reason why I call him a mystic man or a miracle man. As I had already explained that man always die as a man but not as human. This is one example where this Mouna Muni had all in his hands to become Living God but refused instantly to die as human.

EVOLUTION

"Doctor, will you explain on evolution of brain, I remember you using this word very often in your counselling sessions."

Very interesting question you asked. The evolutional trail of man is extraordinary. From Homo erect to Homo sepia, we do not possess any file documentation to prove how human brain evolved. Each layer of our neo-cortex to develop has taken millions of years. If you want to understand the pre-wired and preprogrammed nature of our brains strength, you should know that the one cubic cm of our brain is equal to all the super computers of LHC of CERN put together. Hence, could you imagine the artificial intelligence? Word "homo" after all is meant for man's "wise" nature. Hence, for each wise attitude of a man add automatically a new neuron in his brain. For humans forebrain to add a hundredth of an mm thick brain layer would require millions of years of human' wise behaviors of their cumulative knowledge. The mass of brain is always disproportional to the wisdom of man or in other words the man who has large brain need not always be wise. It is also not true that a brain weighing thousand five hundred grams is more intelligent. Whatever the brain size the numbers of neurons are almost same except in a brain, which weighs nine hundred grams below as in our mentally retarded people. You have many studies where brain shrinks through the aging process but still maintain the same number of neurons if cognition of this person does not get affected.

You are puzzled to now, how my Open Meditation would add a neuron in your brain. Before I answer this question, let me tell you that each neuron does have ten thousand to fifteen thousand synaptic connections. Each synapse is like micro-junction where signals ends and another signal starts afresh with another neuron. These signals passed unaltered due to the presence of normal functioning neurotransmitters. Any alteration in the quantity and quality of neurotransmitters would lead to improper signal transfer. When this happens, the signal processing system would not function properly. When processing is not all right in a factory then the product of this factory would not be good. Our minds basic products are good thoughts, good work, good feeling and reasonable wish or will. When these products do not possess ISI mark then automatically man would become wayward in his functional capacity. If it is uncontrollable, you are a psychiatric patient or same under your control then you are C by 2. Nevertheless, many of us do not belong to these two groups because this group pose normalcy outwardly but inwardly they are immoral, unethical and uncomprehending. Hence, we are worried about this large group in which many of us tuck in. Exactly here my Open Meditation works because if I am immoral, unethical and incomprehensible then I do not allow my new brain to develop an extra neuron but adding a neuron is a possibility if I am transparent, pleural and true proprietor.

You might ask how this could be possible. Listen carefully; addition of extra neuron takes place if my immorality changes to morality, if I practice ethical practice, if I am observable, if I am elaborative and if I am more comprehending. When my comprehension increases my patience increases. With each minute of my patience, I am acquiring extra knowledge. This knowledge would allow me to realize. This realization does require more connections in the brain. These sets of realizations allow our protein to prepare a neuron with myriads of connections to neighbouring neurons. This is how body would allow our neo-cortex to have an extra neuron. Now you tell me, all these things are possible by closing my eyes. No, it is not possible because by closing eyes and meditating I am deeply engrossed to myself. My Open Meditation would help you to mix well with the environment around you. The signals pass from outside when our eyes are open. With this dictum I assert my Open Meditation technique allow our brain to have more and more neuronal connection. Say IQ of 98 would increase to IQ 104. Therefore, by one extra neuron in your brain would increase six quotients up. There is a reason for me to mention six.

With my little knowledge on the computers, for binary language to arrive any principle letter or character you require six questions "yes" or "no" type. For example, "yes" is "0" and "no" is "1." We have to feed these six bits to the computer for it to recognize the letter or the character. Let us say that in the world we have only six letters, now the brain has the capacity to juggle these letters by its pre-wired network roughly around one million information. Likewise, for three hundred words, brain has the information up to three hundred multiplied by six million words of information. This amounts to one big encyclopaedia. Similarly, for three thousand words, it would come around to one thousand such encyclopaedias of information. In the sense, each nucleotide of our gene has the capacity of one billion information to store. It is amazing to find the information by such lacks and lacks of nucleotides stored in the double helical ladder of DNA. Now find out the amount of information we have in our brain. Generally, man uses only four percent of such information in his life time just like what we observe the matter as *Vyktha* (seen) of *Ago Brahman* (universe). This is also around four percent. Other ninety-six percent of information of ours would come only when how many signals enter our body. Man is preprogrammed super social animal designed by the creator to accept always-good signals by default. If by chance any bad signal tries to enter the body, it would automatically close its gate for such obnoxious signals. Presently this fast-paced informative technological world for unknown reasons our body lost its automatic closure system and allows all good and bad signals. Fine, with all these odds, once again the creator is compassionate to human that his brain designed and has programmed to activate its servomechanism to cut down the spikes and sharp wave's activity, which could otherwise precipitate seizure attack by such bad signals. Still, this world is full of colours and lots of *Maaya* (illusions). The signals that emit from these sources are so strong, it surpasses the sieve and servomechanism of human system, which would lead to some known and unknown mind and body ailments. This is also a deterring factor, nudging the hid information's in the genes. Hence, when we develop a system to strengthen our filter mechanisms strong, we are able to bring more than four percent information. This is how good information entered would unfurl already existing stored information in to only good. This is a possibility only when we practice Yoga. The good signals a man could allow only when he is awake and aware with his eyes wide open, not by closing eyes. This is exactly the previously mentioned Open Meditation technique of mine is all about.

In my Open Meditation, one should be aware and searching. Without indulging in searching, nothing enters the mind and searcher should have a capacity to observe the dynamic world. This is how a seeker would search Good and leaves Bad. I am one in my *Mouna* (silence) kept talking with my four-quarters of my consciousness (Dr, Prof, literate and a spiritualist) to arrive for my own metaphors and adjectives. I think my discussion along with four of them would have allowed a new Neuron to develop in my brain (not sure of this). You try my method of discussion; probably this would help you to have a new neuron in your brain.

ANGRY YOUNG POET

"Doctor, are you sure, your Open Meditation always helps those who practice your method?"

Yes, answer is simply "no." Kindly have patience to listen to the story what I explain to you now. Before coming to the point, I will brief you something on behalf of parents. You can decide whether it will be a "duty" or "responsibility." In my Parivarthana (the change), I have explained in length about the *Kaama* (the lust) from which no one would escape the lust in the chapter *Das* or *Daasa.* To fresh up, it is the neuro-chemical mechanism, which makes man total void to produce children for the world to experience. With all said and done, sometimes my Open Meditation does have no role or have some role. In my practice, I have seen, especially in families irrespective of nuclear or extended, neither a family member of these families nor another family member of the same family would listen or understand each other. Here mutual respect and their purchase of time would solve many of their problems. Hence, observation and patience are the tools of my Open Meditation Technique. Many of us use different technique like arguments, quarrelling and finally assault. These are negative attributes of life leading to problems in future. The best thing would be to escape from the point of fire, and to cool in his or her closed air-conditioned room. This is best technique but it would not give all the necessary solution. You be there or live in fire but try to find the instant coolant. The time is the coolant.

Many times impulsiveness is a spark to explode. Therefore, opposite of impulsiveness is patience. Hence, "patience" is the one tool of many tools in my technique of Open Meditation. I have narrated a story in my pervious first English book Parivarthana (the change) about how burns teach the meditation. Nothing helps our skin to regenerate but it is only the time. To add to my statement I explain a story to you. How a specific personality trait could be burning issue. If you had a chance to go through *Chanakya Neethi*, he explains what an incompetent son could do to the family, further he says that this son is like dried up tree when ignite on a spark just burns in to ashes in minutes, similarly many members in the family would burn their families without notice.

My doctor friend's friend was having a "paranoid personality" and wife was having "passive aggressive personality." Being a psychiatrist to my knowledge both personalities do not fuse together. They are like "snake" and "mongoose." Whenever he hisses, she would snarl. As days passed he decided hissing would help no good, hence he decided to spew venomous poison "infidelity" a single paranoid thought not amounting to delusion. When they had reached this stage wife had stopped passiveness but exhibited aggression. Basically she is a girl from orthodox Hindu extended family who was taught by her parent's that she has to swallow all bitter pills in her course of married life. She decided to turn her aggression inwards. She would have thought that her husband's paranoid problem was secondary to her beauty. Hence, out of an impulsive behavior she poured kerosene in front of her husband and lit herself. She sustained fifty-five percent burn injuries. Husband was speechless; his compassion outraced his paranoid taunts. Immediately he took her to the hospital. From few lakhs of rupees and few months of her stay in the corporate hospital, he is lucky to have his wife back. He bestowed with double whammy. He lost his money and earning time. He left with two wounds, wife burn and his heartburn. His paranoid ideas and thoughts dampen and wife was relieved of his insults but left with scars over face and chest including bottom with a functionary opening to meet her nature calls. What an irony with tyranny for just a hiss and snarl. This problem could be prevented in spite of his paranoid picture and her passive aggressive features. A psychiatric intervention would have required if his problem was of a delusional disorder. Unfortunately, it was not a delusional disorder. Here my Open Meditation technique probably would have helped them by just entering each mind without hiss and snarl.

What this statement would mean? It would mean that he understands his wife's trust and aggression-less by her would have prevented all. A timely talk, mutual discussion after knowing the pulse of each other and ventilating their emotions with the persons they know well would have prevented this trauma. Here is a situation where in spite of their *Yoga Asana's* and Meditation could not have prevented the impulsive behavior. What I mean here is that both cannot do the same at a time but definitely they could have used certain tools of my Meditation Technique at the same time. These tools are not my invention but they are already there, it is for the warring factions to purchase these tools. To purchase tools of life does need certain period and that period is *Samyama* or the patience. Sorry, I have used certain derogatory words to my friend's friend but whatever has happened in this story is a true story.

There is another condition where my technique would be a flop. I have once again a story for you. A adolescent boy who was in engineer second semester with a borderline personality (defiant, demanding and deviant) would come home in the absence of his father threatening mother of dare consequences if she was not support him to offer money for his enjoyments. He would never open his mouth for the money he would spend. As soon as he comes home mother is scared, her senses would get frozen, jaw's chatters, there would be derealisation and depersonalisation affect in her, she would shiver and would have palpitation with profuse sweating because he had destroyed all the electronic equipments in his house and had threatened with a knife to kill her. Now, you tell how this mother's mind could enter son's mind. She would offer whatever he would have asked for to get relieved of the situation. She left with only fear, curse and dejection. Father had rejected him, sister was scared and mother was depressed. Imagine a family of four members with these characters. Whom should we blame now, their genes or the creator? The only time she would meditate was when he was not coming home for the reason of enjoying marihuana with his friends. They tried all their methods to manage him by visiting numerous Gods and doctors with no remedy. This saga continued for years and years and had not he completed his professional course, mother got diabetes and hypertension, father had a stroke and sister got married and left home, now he left alone abused to multiple substances. They tried long stay home, deaddiction centres and frequent hospital admissions. Their pocket emptied and parents were praying God that God would help their destiny. God bestowed his blessings when he got killed in a road accident, as he was high with the substance he had abused to. Mother improved with her diabetes and her hypertension was controlled. Father was happy in spite of his neurological problem as he was managing his family with the pension what he was getting and sister had a sigh of relief living comfortably with her spouse. Now tell me my Open Meditation had any role in this condition. For a point of fact what could have managed their vows. Their entire problem solved not by *Yoga Asana, Pranayana* or *Meditation*, but by their wards' death my friend. It is the close proximity with Yama helped their family. Do not think Yoga did not help this family, it has helped. The true Yoga for the family was their son's demise. In this tragedy mother could not meditate whatsoever to enter her son's mind but her son as young remained in her heart presumably forever.

My Yoga does not help the poor. Poor in this world live happily with their daily earnings. They earn and eat on the day-to-day basis. They work daily and sleep comfortably. The true Yoga here is that they should not succumb to alcohol and smoking. Here what I mean Yoga is education. Explaining these peasants with the side effects alcohol and smoking that would induce. Yoga is to provide poor children of our society good education and with better living standards. Therefore, here Yoga is not for forcibly to impose *Yoga Asana* but to provide the basic human needs.

June 21st of every year is been celebrated as Yoga International Day. For me, it is not, it should be the International Day Of Yoga Asana. Do not confuse with Yoga to Yoga Asana. Yoga is different from Yoga Asana. It is for the people of the world to awake, to know what actually the definition of Yoga is about. When the "health" is explained in defined terminologies by World Health

Organisation, Similarly, when United Nations Organisation had agreed on Yoga, it is for this organization to define Yoga in an acceptable way by the people all over the world. My point is Yoga is been explained rather than defined. As the definition of Health been brought under our curriculum Yoga too have the opportunity. Until now, Yoga loosely explained by different religions sectors, but by the fact, different set of people explained differently in the same religion.

Frankly speaking, I do not know what made certain people to perform this day as Yoga Day. There is nothing Yoga here, it appears like common drill program as any school boys do. Hence, *Yoga Asana* day here is also a farce day. As the days progress people demand for Kungfu Day, Kaliapattu Day, Ushu Day and like on and like forth including Day Of Crime. In this Day Of Crime, a crime is not a crime. This is exactly happening with our politicians, they have asked us to honour Yoga, allowing their own people to exercise corruption, helping discarded criminals and cheating the people of their own country. Yoga is not a business. Yoga stands for knowledge. The seeker who practices Yoga is Yogi. Yogi is a man of contemplation. This knowledge of contemplation in him would help him to detach. This detachment allow him to reach little *Moksha* (liberation). In this *Moksha*, he would see *Ananda* (peace and solace). This is what *Vedantha* says. Broadly, the above statement could be put in simple equation as "*Sath* (truth) *Chith* (mind) *Ananda* (solace)." The Supreme Court of India has taken cognizance to the effect that the Yoga is not a proprietor ship. Yoga is the age old traditional teachings of *Sanathana Dharma*(ancient scriptures). Hence, no one in this world have any claim on Yoga as their patency. I would prefer the Yoga Day should commemorated as Pathnajali Day. We are good at forgetting sages and *Gurus* who have taught us good.

I would like to remind you, how this Yoga of this Yoga Day is different from simple exercise like drill exercise performing when we were students. It is heart reckoning to notice that today the schools sanctioned without a playground to play. Today in our school curicullum "physical training" class been abolished. In this hour of play, unnecessarily children head been filled with subjects. I am sure; such pressure would burst the brain of our children. Today our children stressed. Uncompromising stress has driven these children for easier ways to end their life like suicide, substance abuse and indulging in deviant behavior. All children would require a "vent" to vent out their stresses. The best way children could vent out their stresses is in the playgrounds. Hence, imagine a school without a playground.

My Open Meditation does not help few. For example an adolescent in this competitive society who is dogged by many obsessions. He is unable to enter any ones brain including his parents due to the quantum of obsession he possess. Many obsessions are obsessions of passing without reading, his obsessions of achieving without effort and his obsessions of procuring material without working, etc., adolescent obsessions would create ripples in his mind for minor incidences from his surroundings. These would have led to irritability with maladjustments. Adolescent forgets that everything settles with reading, effort and working but what an adolescent lacks is the patience. Adding patience here is the work of Open Meditation. This "patience" is not available against material. It has to imbibe by learning. The true Meditation in my type of meditation is by the parents to know their adolescents with patience. As long as the patience is maintained well by the parent's, the life clicks, otherwise get destroyed. Hence, indirectly my Open Meditation would help these adolescents. The adolescents' happiness comes after money, which I cannot give, so adolescent's irritability remain still they earn money. Money comes late, hence their Medicament too. I would rather expect somebody to discover super buffer between "irritability" and the "money" so as to experience minimal bruises by adolescents'. After all Meditation is "self-medication to our disturbed emotions."

Today, talented young generations perceive this competitive world fearful. Therefore, youths are left with confusion and also allow themselves anxiety to stay, naturally hate is a principle factor and there you have irritability. When youth hosts all these attributes, he finds difficult to channelize out the heat he has in him through proper outlets. In this situation, the youth lodge with dogmatic negative principles. Many of them are obsessed with their future and principally sex. In these set of conditions, my Open Meditation has neither has any role nor has some role. Preamble to my statement I had a young boy of twenty-one years with irritability, aggressiveness, blaming and destroying. This behavior of him led mother to consult a local psychiatrist in his earlier place where his father was working. There he was forced to take antipsychotics. The side effects made him to sit for his exams twice. He passed the exam after stopping the drugs on his own. However, his behavior never altered. They transferred to my place as his father was working in a government office. They wanted a consultation. They approached me. He was on mood stabilizers. After detailed history taking, I found that his aggression was for not identifying his talent. For all his abusiveness and blame games, his family members were the target. For all his aggressive destruction, the house electronic equipments were the target. His mother had explained me about his reading habit who reads always philosophical and many English books. His writing habits were like scribbling in a paper, squeezing the same and throwing the scribbled paper to dust bin. He is a talented debater. Always debates against the societal ills, worshiping practices and customs followed by us and on the God. In his class, he was recognized as reclusive, exclusive, elusive and delusive. At some time of his mental state examination, he was on different mood stabilizers to control his aggression. One day his mother asked him regarding his recent write up to show to me. I really fascinated by his literary poem,

A POEM OF A POET

Thousands of water flow to the sea,

Hundreds of tears reach the ground,

Bullets of bloodshed down the life,

Broken glasses cannot fix the feelings,

Doubt the love against your love,

Can't grow a flower of rose to one,

Leaving all out the rest at the end,

I am going mad inside like a blend,

Will you forget me from the past?

Till you forgive me at very last,

I am a dead old man to die alone,

Never to say true to go lay alone,

Writing the write, wrote, is it not a life to lead,

Writing an unwritten, wrote, is it life to cease?

I am an anonymous poet I am an anonymous poet.

Waiting for an anonymous duet,

A song in to a reality, broken and shaken,

A hate of sacred to live or die,

I goanna sleep of daydreams,

Beaming a past and future,

I am a past in future from present, but I am continuous, but I am continuous….

Is it not worth mentioning this poem of him?

Next is THE HOST

Threatened love serves most,

Frightened light glows most,

Light above lies is bright,
Understood I a dark mat,
Every man has host of his own,
Condensed rains showers all over,
Not every grain has due of rain,
No, it is not over,
I am a host of unknfown,
Sings bone, searching body that fits my host of unknown,
Death comes very near to us,
Inside tells me a lot to tell,
Rings a bell of hell,
Till the trail I am known, I am known.
What a poem……

Here, tell me why this boy would require my Open Meditation. He had already Hosted inside him the Meditation but what he would require is recognition and a proper channelization of his work. It is teaching my Open Meditation to him and his parents probably would help to come out of his aggression. I feel a structured oriented counselling would also help him a lot along with on and often mood stabilizers.

DREAMS

"Doctor, tell me what my dream is all about?"

Very interesting, yesterday I dreamt myself as a thief. Woke up immediately and remembered *Janaka Maharaja.* I always say, dream is a living state where you are going to be exposing your true colours. You yourself are the witness for all your deeds. In your dreamless state, you are masked. When not dreaming you feign wise, where as in a dream, dream do not bother about you, you are naked in the dream state. The punishment for the torture you did when you are wakeful and pleasure you enjoyed for the deeds you performed, all these images get distorted in your dreams. The pictures in dream, all though visualized, as a movie is not continuous or connected. You should know that in a dream state, you have no thoughts, thoughts are blocked. Only images you have. Thoughts are there when you are wakeful. When you are awake, your thoughts are connected. In deep sleep state neither you have images nor thoughts. In the dreams, the connections as I said earlier are of disconnections but still connected. How? Listen- you trouble someone when you are awake, dream punish you. This punishment you cannot enjoy when you are awake but dream allows you to enjoy the torture because you are rightfully entitled to this torture. Whatever you are not able to possess during your life, dream try to offer the same to you. You name what you do not have in the wakeful state; you have same in your dream wholly. Hence, dream always asks you to be happy. If dreams were not there man would have gone mad. This is exactly the reason why if someone has no sleep and not experienced the dreams is termed neurotic. When you are awake, having dream is called as daydream. Dreams are movies in which your "self" is the actor and your "will possessor" would be the actress. Frankly, your wife is not the actress. This movie is not continuous, it is disjointed, one moment you are here and next moment you are somewhere. You are naked, actress is also naked too, half visualized, one moment top, another moment bottom and the movie is not complete. This movie is distorted which lacks good direction, directed by you alone in which always yourself being projected as a villain. Dream is an absurd state because what you do not have during your awake state you have these things always in your dreams. This is true because I have experienced, it is pseudo-phantom experience, not a true phantom, a psychiatric word experienced when awake. Example for this phenomenon being, experiencing the intactness of a limb after it is been amputated due to some disease or in trauma. In my case, I never had any phantom phenomenon when I am awake about my rectum which was removed earlier for my tumor, I experienced extensively pseudo-phantoms in my dreams defecating jolly wholly. I enjoy dreams; dreams pumped my life tempo until now. When I am awake, it is really painful when I compare myself to others who have their rectums intact but immediately I realize a young married male patient who was lying beside my bed with multiple cysticercoids with intractable seizures and behavioral changes secondary to organic brain changes in the hospital where I was admitted. Even today, I keep getting the thoughts of his wife plight in front of me. I feel

I am better rather feeling best. It is all in the comparison, which makes you more composed which brings succour in your life. Look always down, never look up my friend. I never say that you should not look up. Lookup when you met all the obligations of your life. Lookup when your Ego is down. Lookup when you are saviour. Lookup when you are the good model. Lookup when you are aspiring to do something to the society. This is what we call as *Saadhana* (little achievement). Until then, you remain as a humble human.

I had a dream, interesting dream. After arduous long drive in my car felt like rest my car wayside a *Beeda* stall attached Bar. We quest our strain, I do not know how many pints, wife is beside, I know not how many she had. Past midnight, I was asleep, nothing wake me up. I woke up past five early morning listing to my own different music album contrary to what I listen regularly which already was inside my music system. Doors half open, eyes half open I see many human forms dark long hands and legs with few Halloweens, I woke up and am wholly awake, once again all in dreams, wife is still sleeping by my side. For my scream, the creepy forms slide and moving away, Halloweens flying away, more I scream more, they pacing away more and more. It is all in dreams, my shouts are out of my fear and these forms had not armed to kill me or maim me. The fear in me was enough to harm me.

There is this time when I wake up, with my wife still sleeping in my real bed; I get out from my bed fresh and happy for finding an answer to all our ills; I felt that the fear in us is the root cause. I thought Gods and Evils are same with no weapons to save us or kill us respectively, it is all our fear we harbour to say that there are Gods and Evils.

The fear is there for the sound, not for the image. Ghost without skirmish sound is not Ghost.

With this *Vedanthic* mind took few steps to the room and peeped where my Grandson sleeping to say good morning expecting a tiny smile from his tiny mouth to refresh my mind from my past and for a happy day to pass. Toddlers smile and weep in their dreams; theirs are un-contaminated minds, for our smiles from our heart they smile and for our smiles which are not from our heart they weep. It is a simple equation of truth. Can anybody tell me what infant has in his mind to smile or to weep in his or her dreams? His or hers smiles and weeps reflect our smiles whether from our heart or not.

"Doctor, possessing dream is it a hallmark for an achiever?"

Possessing a dream for any achiever is a myth. If somebody asks you to possess a dream, he is a dreamless man. Possessing dream in a wakeful state is psychopathological state as in Schizophrenia. If a scientist says that he had a dream, he is a fool. His out of blue experience is not a dream. It is a flash of light like lightening. The true pioneer of Rocket Technology, Goddard never dreamt the energy lifting the rocket in to space. It was his out of blue experience experienced when he was on the top of a branch of one regular tree in his backyard, which used by him to climb this tree every day. On the top of this tree he thought of travelling to Mars. He felt, it was his energy made him to climb up the tree; he used same analogy in his work that the energy would take him to reach Mars one day. He termed this energy as fuel. Today the rocket fuel technology would go by his name. The dreams are not lightning's. The dreams cannot be good thoughts either. Dreams are automatic images only. Thoughts are expressive but dreams are not expressive. If these dreams are expressive then you are caught and you are entitled to have punishment as per the Law of Land. Because, whatever you had dreams is to the tunes of your "Will." Your Will never listens to you. This will of yours asks for a bumpy wetly girl. You are deceiving your wife. If you express this dream to your wife then once again you are caught. You are punished not by Statutory Law but by the Law of Marriage. Hence, never tell your dreams to your wife or to any close person. Let us all dream for a good mental hygiene.

Coming to Janaka Maharaja (mighty Vedic King) who doused off on his crown while there was a deliberation in his *Asthana* (palace) regarding social issues of his *Rajya* (kingdom) seemed to have dreamt that still he being a King is starving. Yes, I am right, because this King was the actor in his own dreams. As I have told you, you are living when you are awake so also in your dream state. Hence dead do not dream. If you do not dream, you are dead (you live with mental disorders). This King wakes up to his dreams with perspiration and confusion. He immediately comes out from his sleep with shakes and shivers. He had explained to his *Manthri* (caretaker) about his dream state. It was just a coincidence that he had this dream in the afternoon lunchtime. This king was known for his prowess and nobleness. He wanted to know the truth behind his dream state. He addresses to his *Manthri* to bring a Brahmin who could explain his dream state. Many Sages and Masters came to his *Asthana* to explain the dream but this King somehow was not satisfied. He was sleepless because he could not dream from that day of his dreams as beggar begging for food. He is either not come out from his anxiety, fear and confusion. This king had sent the messengers to all the nook and crannies.

One odd-looking man approached a soldier who was restless to find a Brahmin for his master. He asked the reason for his restlessness. Soldier explained the reason regarding his fear. This ordinary odd-looking man told the soldier that he would crack all the Kings questions. Soldier could not believe this odd man and just refused to take him to the King. This humble peasant who had eight knots on eight joints pressurized soldier to take him to the King. With reluctance, this soldier took him to the King. After looking at this man, King scolded soldier for bringing him. Unfazed and defiant gentle man addresses the king

"O lord of life the Janaka the King, ask me questions. It is not my body answers your questions but the knowledge I possess answers your question. I am able to enter your mind and see the tension, the fear, the confusion you have for the question you harbour. My wise mind and un-contaminated vision can feel and see the questions you possess." This is exactly my Open Meditation does. It is the way to enter others mind unhindering and unscathed to feel and know what people have in their minds. This is exactly Dr Abdul Kalam preached. He had always asked young to acquire knowledge. What I would like to explain you is that if you have the knowledge which you got de facto or learnt, would enable you to follow and practice of my Open Meditation easily.

After addressing King Janaka by Sage Ashta Vakra would go further explains what dichotomy lies between one's "I" and his own "Self-consciousness." He teaches him the afflictions, affections and affirmations. When King started feeling the pain, insecurity and bad effect of such attachments, he begs Sage Ashtavakra to get relieve of his ignorance. Sage Ashtavakra was pleased with the obeisance of King Janaka offered to him and this is how Sage teaches this King the path of detachment and liberation.

FUNCTIONAL GODS

"Who is this God Doctor?"

O my God! God is God. Evil is evil. God is not evil. This equation is a simple primary class equation. My father said there is God, my mother believed this God, relatives prayed to the God, wife worshiped the God and so God is there all along. Now I cannot say there is no God. To explain, the God you mentioned is my projected mindset. This is an object reality, which you and I cannot explain. Hence, according to me, God could be defined as "As long as something is not explainable is God." When the true source of the matter is unexplainable by present science, the particle of the matter is called God's particle. As long as I am not able to link or connect the true nature between man and God, the God would exist. Listen carefully what I say:

In our Hindu culture, on all our day-to-day auspicious transactions we offer hundred rupees plus one rupee as advance. This is just an example. Now my idea is that what makes us to pay hundred one rupees "odd" instead of "even" hundred rupees? Nobody would accept hundred "even" as advance but they insist to add another rupee to this hundred to make it "odd." I was amazed to find this ritual among us. I could not get answer from anyone. Hence, I tried to search the reason behind this compulsion. I found the reason, which may not taste to reader's palate but still worth explaining. The major difference of opinion between present religions is how many Gods each religion has. For a matured man, this argument is idiotic. As we do not have the maturity this argument stands the testimony to kindle and kill. For me this God is amazing, because I discovered God on my own. Approximately in Hindu religion we have thirty-three thousand crores Gods. This number is a peanut compared to the loss of amount when all the fraud amount put together by our political scamsters. My point of argument is that why we do not have thirty-three crores and one God. When I start searching for the answer for this disparity, I have an amazing reason. The explanation is this-

"How many objects universe possesses?"

"Countless or Infinite numbers."

"Can you count?"

"No."

If I start counting objects in this universe, I would find thirty-three thousand crores and one objects. The same analogy holds good for our judiciary. "Justice is delayed is justice denied," when same justice is not delivered "justice is dead." Therefore, justice to the numbers cannot be justified in the Law. When truth to belief has no value in justice, same analogy holds good for the countable objects in this universe. Justice cannot disapprove my number of objects. You asked me to count and I did the same. Now objects are all right, what about Gods, we are interested at them. Here lies the parody, here meaning to God is just to function but not to feel or experience. When God is not felt, how one say that there is God. For a rationalist there is no God, for a believer there is God, who is unable to show but for a spiritualist there exist a God, which is functional. There is not much difference between a spiritualist and a scientist.

Both would experience out of the blue experiences. They also called otherwise as constructive schizophrenics. I am happy if you call me constructive schizophrenic. Destructive schizophrenics are dangerous to our society like terrorists who have harboured delusions of grandeur. Coming to "function" being a God, according to me God is a mere connection between two objects connecting the whole world undisturbed. The connection is to function. To put same in very simple words man is there as long as earth is there. Men ploughs the land, sowed the seed, grows the grain, in turn eat by men. Hence, the process of ploughing is God. The process of seeds thrown on ploughed land is God. The process by which the grown grain harvested is God. The process of processing the raw grains is God. The process of cooking the grain is God. The process of putting processed grain on the plate is God and eating the same is God.

Common friend, I bet I have thousands and thousands of explanations on these functions, which are God-like. Therefore, automatically you have thirty-three thousand crores Gods between thirty-three crores and one objects in this universe. Briefly, the function, the symbiosis and the eco link between each living and non-living object is a God; hence crores and crores of living and non-living objects are there in this universe. Between them, crores and crores of function takes place at any given point of time. Therefore, Gods are everywhere around us to bring the harmony, wealth and well-being of the world at large. Therefore, no object on this earth goes waste. No living object in this earth goes waste. This is the exact teachings of Lord Buddha the *Vipaasana.* Lord Buddha never called himself as God you know. He said you are God when you drop your ignorance. This is Munduka Upanishath's teaching. This Adi Shankaracharya taught us. It is the submission of "I" to his "Self" makes him the God. The love is God, the compassion is God, the forgiveness is God, so be compassionate and find the God everywhere friend.

GODS MUSIC

"Doctor you said God is everywhere. My friend tells me that Music is God. How music could be God?"

Sure, to experience music of God is vital, whereas music of harmony is a science, which we have to discover. Now listen, the age of our earth could be some few billions years old. The modern science has apparent answers for the origin of our earth and for its nature of float in the sea of *Brahman* (universe). While knowing mysticism Ignorant man opens his mouth, astronomer shuts his mouth. For me this earth and universe are mystifying. I am really a proud product of this earth. When Neitze questions the very purpose of our life, I question myself that being a product of this Mother Nature what little I could do to her. In this search of doing something to this Mother Earth I cannot synthesis O_2 (oxygen), drink CO_2 (carbon dioxide) and swallow plastic. Hence, I can pray harmony of nature's survival. Frankly, I have neither music nor any instrument to please my Mother Earth. This is possible only when I listen to nature's natural orchestra. However, I do not possess such ears to listen to her song. Mother Nature bestowed me the super brain. My brain could do only knowing, to know the Mother Earth fully. It is humanly impossible to get in to the roots of Mother Earth, hence whatever I know about Mother Earth I should be obedient, obeisant and oblivious to her.

I have explained earlier the God. This God to whom I have explained does not make any noise. When this God is mute, how can I hear music? Still God could be vibrating. The vibration does not pinch our tympanic membrane, but definitely, this vibration would kindle our knowledge. Hence, to hear this music of God, I should be a knower. To explain little, as each function between two given objects in this world is a God, which is subtle, the music I now narrate is not just subtle God but speaking God. This God does not speak but sings. This is called Music Of God. This earth, which was a speck of hot liquid magna, fired out from a possible Big Bang several billion years ago. As this Earth had exceptional ardent journey from its source of its origin ultimately could come to a point of halt within its axis and definite path in this present Universe. In this process core of the earth remained as hot liquid, intermediate molten magna and outer strong hot rocks cooled, condensed as hard outer crest. Though they are separate but with various vents between them, these three separate entities began to function as one. Between the crest, the water and the hot liquid magna there emits a sound, sound of music. Several kilometres down the pacific sea on the ring of fire through various vents hot gas, molten liquid kept oozing out in to the bottom of sea. In this process there comes of an enchanting and remarkable frequencies of *naada* (music notes). To hear this music you have to drown six kilometres down from sea surface where the pressure is around thousand six hundred times more to earth's surface. To explain same if I reach this bottom unequipped I crushed to paper.

This process of spewing toxic sulphur and other minerals with high temperature is good medium for planktons to grow and multiply in trillions and trillions. In turn, enriched planktons attract lakhs of marine life to feed. The race of dolphins, the trumpet of blue whales, the majestic sounds of killer whales, elegant penguins, chirping sea gulls, splashing fish, happy coral bed, dancing innumerable marine living fauna, you and I could see the Natures charm. The Mother Nature feeds these unsustainable marine animals. While feeding Mother sings a song to the tunes of the happiness these animals, undergo. This is music of God.

Several thousands of miles away the parched lands, which fail to kiss the rain from millions of years does not keep quiet. This land also lends its helping hand to the humankind. Mother Nature is so magnanimous to take care of its children. The bursting and speeding sand storm with full of sand flakes rich in calcium, magnesium, iron, silicon and other natural minerals are carried sky route by clouds promptly enrich the lakhs of hectares of tropical forest of South America for six months of unrelenting music to the tunes of monsoon. Land of South great forest is happy and thankful to the music and the nutrients it has received from the North parched barren land. This is music of God.

After rain stops when sun finds its rays through the thick forest roof tops, fresh and agile plants sprouts enjoying and dancing. Billions of fresh twigs spread across lakhs of hectares cannot wait for the Carbon Dioxide available in the space. After consuming enormous amount of CO_2 fresh and young plants are so kind to release tons and tons of Oxygen to the space. The blowing and whistling wind bring cheers to crores of people all around the world to enjoy the Oxygen the only source to live and progress. This is music of God.

Next in monsoon the rains takes all vegetative soil to waters of great Amazon forest to tow the rich nutrients in to the great depths of sea floor. This vegetative nutrient allows once again the planktons to dance by the tunes of mud, slash and dirt spruit (streams). The planktons multiply in billion and trillion for the lakhs of marine animals to feed once again. This saga of Mother Nature is relentless as millions of years passed, true to the future too. The toxic fumes keep spewing from the core of Mother Earth through mountains of volcano bringing fresh nutrients to the ground for human life to survive. Human toxicity curtailed as toxic fumes soaked by trillions and trillions of water molecules to form huge mineral clouds for the vast tropical forests situated thousands of miles away. In these dense forests, the dance of Carbon Dioxide utilization and Oxygen release would take place in the midst of sprouting green forest playing mystique music of gaseous exchanges. My point is God does not possess the eyes to see the forest orchestra comprising sprinkling rain, blowing wind and mountains singing. God's have no ears to listen to the music produced by frogs, listen to chirping birds and hear the roaring lions. Hence, it is you who possess eyes and ears to enjoy the strings of connecting music. It is you, who has to have the prayers, Praarthana of not throwing plastic, Praarthana of not spiting on the ground, Praarthana of not littering the space with garbage, Praarthana of saving the trees, Praarthana of keeping the forests viable, Praarthana of saving animals from their extinction etc. This is the Music of God.

MEDITATION V/S MEDICATION

"Doctor, I am confused on medication or meditation. Kindly explain?"

No, there is nothing to be confused. What is the confusion, dear friend? "The self-medications to your emotions without medicines are the meditations." Medication is by the doctor, meditation is by the knower. Doctor can be a knower. Doctor need not be a spiritualist. Spiritualism is for knowing. You should make a difference from knowing to knower. While knowing you are attached to this world, whereas knower is a person who has no attachments. Best way of putting across, teacher is a person of knowing and master is a person of known. I will make you clear from this Tao story.

Today we have internet with many social web sites. It had happened that in one of these social websites "Sun" had an opportunity to make friendship with "Cold." They had regular chats in spite of millions and millions of miles away. They became good friends and there was not a single day spent with no chat. Somehow, "Cold" wanted to meet "Sun." "Cold" with help of NASA (National Aeronautical Space Association) after paying millions of dollars left to see "Sun." When "Cold" reached "Sun," "Cold" said "What a transformation in me." They had good pleasantries, spent days celebrating with frequent parties, enjoyed the subtle world of "Sun" and finally "Cold" requested "Sun" to have his hospitality in return. "Sun" being heavy and big just drops inside the cave where "Cold" is residing. "Cold" is happy receiving "Sun" with all state honours and gun salute. "Sun" as usual spent lot of days with "Cold." There were celebrations with late night parties of belly dance to revelry and tequila. Finally "Sun" felt, it is time to leave. Both of them hugged and kissed before departing. Before "Sun" said bye bye, "Cold" did not resist asking a question "How was my hospitality, did you find any change in you?," "Sun" said "absolutely no change, I did not find any change staying with you." Moral of the story is that for the master "Sun" there is nothing to change but for the teacher "Cold" there is everything to change. Hence, a Doctor could be a teacher or master. Adopting the process of spirituality would change a teacher to master. Spirit is a subject for a person to study whereas spirituality is a process to adopt. This is ever ending saga because no person can be Spiritual. Therefore, person could be a person of knowing or a person of knower. The "Spirit" subject is vast which you have to find in the BRAHMAN between Sun and Cold. The art of knowing is the meditation and your master is a knower who just nods his head or accepts your learnt "Known," and mind you, he never inks that you are known. In this process of meditation the true medicines (off tablets) for your emotions are three "H," they are humbleness, humanity and humility.

"Doctor, what are the other constructs of good meditation?"

Meditation is a building block with three constructs. These are three "A's. One is Arouse, the second is Aware and the third is Awake." This is exactly the theme of my Open Meditation. In my practice, for all excited patients, I sedate them with anxiolytics or by antipsychotics. Relatives or patients bystanders are very happy because I have knocked him down. After several hours relatives asks me about his feeds. Any amount of counselling would not pacify them regarding his lunch or dinner. Parental drugs would take care of the excited patient for at least twelve hours. As bystander's patience loses my patience too, reach a boiling point. I explain, "Look, food is required for an active person, not for a sedated person under treatment." They think I am Yama who wants to take away his *Athma* to sell same for someone else. All doctors are mature enough take care of their patients through parental route. At sometime, their inability rues the eventuality. No doctor wants to kill a patient. Doctor is not a psychopath (exceptions are the rule). These bystanders have their own mindset regarding their kith and kin. They feel sedated patient would go hypoglycaemic if they do not feed. It is unfortunate; doctors have lost their patients feeding while patients are in drowsy. My point is that eating is a type of Meditation. Now, how could a man on earth eat eatery with his closed eyes? You can do for a while but try eating *Vada* in a plate and *Sambar* in a cup separately. Let me not discuss *Dip Vada*. You know how difficult to quench your hunger with *Vada* and *Sambar* because the eatery you are eating not placed in one plate. Hence, here *OPEN MEDITATION* deals with the geometry of your patience for not spilling and soiling your clothes. Fine, your hunger is taken off, then what next. Tea or coffee, then what? If the *Vada* you ate is tasty, you start meditating more. Here my meditation would mean to know the *Vada* and *Sambar* better. The ingredients, the batter prepared, the oil used, the temperature of this oil, the time taken for roast and similarly making good *Sambar*. All constitutes for a good knowledge on *Vada* and *Sambar*.

This is just an example. If you ask me, what my meditation is, my meditation would be psychiatry not cardiology. In this way, your wife's meditation should be to make *Vada* and *Sambar* in the kitchen. If she is a CEO, she has to meditate to the company in which she is working for. Likewise, you should know your subject well; this would bring down your emotions for a better understanding in your life. You know, our emotion's (expressed motion is emotion) are expressed for not understanding life well. Student is irritable for not knowing his subject well. When you make him understand his mistakes, his emotions come down. This is Meditation. You cannot do this by closing your eyes. You should be knowledgeable to find your mistakes. This is my Open Meditation Technique. In our life, same analogy could be used in various life attributes. Finally, it is our simple observation, observed knowledge; analysing and adaptation of this knowledge would bring the required patience. If we are able to make Open Meditation, a key to success, we can patronize well among our community and we can be patricians in the society.